by Paul Christensen

POETRY:

Old and Lost Rivers (1977)
The Vectory (1981)
Signs of the Whelming (1983)
Weights and Measures (1985)

CRITICISM:

Charles Olson: Call Him Ishmael (1979)
*In Love, In Sorrow: The Complete Correspondence of
    Charles Olson and Edward Dahlberg* (1990)
*Minding the Underworld: Clayton Eshleman and Late
    Postmodernism* (1991)

MINDING THE UNDERWORLD

& CLAYTON ESHLEMAN LATE POSTMODERNISM

PAUL CHRISTENSEN

BLACK SPARROW PRESS

SANTA ROSA   1991

LIBRARY OF CONGRESS CATALOGING-IN-PUBLICATION DATA

Christensen, Paul, 1943-
 Minding the underworld : Clayton Eshleman and late postmodernism
Paul Christensen.
  p. cm.
 Includes bibliographical references.
 ISBN 0-87685-822-1 (cloth) :   — ISBN 0-87685-823-X (signed cloth) :
— ISBN 0-87685-821-3 (pbk.) :
 1. Eshleman, Clayton—Criticism and interpretation. 2. Postmodernism
(Literature)—United States. I. Title.
PS3555.S5Z6   1991
 811'.54—dc20   91-2933
                                                              CIP

To Mary

CONTENTS

Preface   9
Key to Major Texts by Clayton Eshleman   14
Chapter One: Waves of Energy   17
Chapter Two: A Poetics of the Body   77
Chapter Three: Fathers and Sons   127
Chapter Four: "The Descent Beckons"   177
Notes   227
Index   235

PREFACE

The idea for this book came from reading Clayton Eshleman's *Hades in Manganese,* which he had sent me shortly after I had completed editing the correspondence of Charles Olson and Edward Dahlberg, which Eshleman was publishing in the opening issue of *Sulfur.* I was now seeing Postmodernism from the vantage point of Dahlberg's skeptical mind, the doubting genius of midcentury life. Against all of Olson's enthusiasms came Dahlberg's warnings not to lose sight of basic human longings, or the tragic fate of human nature. Dahlberg was the other end of postmodern art, its darker, wizened flesh, and together both men drew a circle around a body of thought whose inmost secrets still eluded me. When I read *Hades in Manganese* in 1982, and then *Fracture* a year later, I sensed a conclusion being reached in those remarkable books, a sum under a circuitous logic that wove its way back into the preceding decades of poetry. Somewhere in those books lay the key to what had motivated one of the most frenzied periods of literary experiment in American cultural history.

I did not want to write another study of the technical and esthetic conundrums of postmodern writing. Nor did I wish to set up a particular writer as the key figure of the era; my aim was to adopt the perspective of one of its leading artists as a means of exploring the esthetic temperament and social conditions of the mid-century, while at the same time allowing myself the freedom to express my own views and perceptions of events as well. While I do not actually put on the identity of Eshleman to examine his times, I generally sympathize with his views and depart from them only when I feel the necessity to establish another, sometimes contrary viewpoint of my own. But Eshleman was a strategic choice for studying an era of poetry; he is one of a group of poets, among whom are Jerome Rothenberg, Robert Kelly, Diane Wakoski, Armand Schwerner and David Antin, whose critical interests and vision arose in the early days of postmodern thought and who have worked out in common many of the main themes of postmodernism in their mature poetry. Though the group itself has long since dispersed, the work of these original "deep imagists" is unusual in American writing for the ground they continue to share and for the mutuality of their depictions of modern, problematic culture. To treat the themes and strategies of Eshleman is, in a way, to deal with all the other figures of his circle as well; despite their individual differences in style, taste, approach, the poetry of these writers follows a program of psychological analysis and of mythopoeic critiques of contemporary life. They are, in my view, the only real extensions of postmodern writing after Olson's generation.

My main intention in writing a book on the new poetry was to find a historical grounding in the era, to show how this seemingly opaque or oblique lyric mode was as responsive and referential to the times as was American literature of a century before. The American renaissance had been goaded into being by the withdrawal of puritanism from American thought and art. Whitman, Emerson, Thoreau, Hawthorne and Melville were redefining life in America after the collapse of a theocratic regime; hence, F. O. Matthiessen's implied comparison to the Italian Renaissance in the title of his formidable study of the era, *American Renaissance.*

I set out to find the withdrawal of a tradition from which Postmodernism could be said to have sprung. My thesis began to form as I traveled around to different outposts of the old British Empire—in New Zealand, Borneo, Malaysia, Singapore—during a year of teaching abroad. At some point it occurred to me that the struggles for an independent voice among ex-colonies bore a remarkable resemblance to the causes and rhetorical strategems used by American writers of virtually the same period. American writers who were turning to their native experience can be seen as participating in a world-wide post-colonial renaissance of native traditions.

The midcentury marked the end of the old-style European empires, and of claims made for the superiority of Western European racial characteristics and beliefs. In a way, European influence was now withdrawing from the world, shrinking to its own continental borders, within which suppressed native traditions were also continuing to voice opposition and separatist emotions. Europe was fracturing, and in the process, the world's diverse cultures were beginning to be heard again. But the emergence of two other empires coincided with this sudden cultural pluralism, and their ominous presence threatened the future of these still-independent and unaligned new states. Russia and the United States had the means for reestablishing hegemonic rule and of enforcing cultural uniformity from their separate centers of power. Was not Japan already forming a miniature American economy in the Far East?

Thus, Postmodernism had two outlooks on the reemergence of native cultures: the one jubilant and full of high expectations for the arts after British and European hegemony withered away; the other saw grave dangers to freedom posed by new imperial aggression against the unaligned nations of the Third World. Charles Olson set Postmodernism in motion as a voice of cultural pluralism in the world. He too would realign himself esthetically to one of empire's most notable victims, Mexico's Aztec civilization and later on Mayan culture as well. But as the Cold War deepened and American imperial interests grew bolder, it became clear that that mood was eroding and a darker, more brooding perspective began setting in. I trace much of this new mood in the work of Eshleman and the writing he collected in *Caterpillar* (1967–1973), then in *Sulfur*, beginning in 1981.

Not until I faced a classroom of undergraduates with these issues did I actually undergo the ordeal in which intuitions and half-perceptions were forced into communicable form. After several months of harrowing abstractness, I recall scribbling on the blackboard Martin Buber's midcentury formulation of dichotomy, I and Thou. I drew a line underneath and repeated the two terms. Above the line was a conscious antipathy between subject and object, of we versus they, human nature versus the rest of nature, Western ethnocentricity versus the Third World. On the plain of consciousness, things divided into rivalries and antagonisms, or simply disintegrated under the glare of analysis and classification. The conscious "I" cast out its otherness and thrived on its exclusionary principle. This history of "I" is the adventures of a predatory, hungry I looking for content to press into service. Under the line was the unconscious, the underworld, where the roots between I and Thou mingled and nourished together, like two trees drawing from the same soil. With our required text in hand, Rothenberg's *Symposium of the Whole,* I quoted various excerpts from Blake, Vico, Duncan, Victor Turner to demonstrate the basic principle of ethnopoetics, that deep within the Thou lay ourselves all along. Only the "I" of consciousness severed relations to others; but in dreams, trances, spells, we found in Thou our own eyes staring back at us. Turner refers to this recognition as the profound reflexivity now coming back into Western thought and art. In Thou lay the "not-not-me," the transcendence of alienation. These words went out to a white audience in which a lone black student sat along the far wall, next to a window.

With undergraduates wide-eyed before you, you don't forfeit the chance to let an idea sink in by repetition. I sailed on with more embellishments on the theme of I-in-Thou. The arts of the last century and more formed an underground pilgrimage between I and Thou, I remarked, as I described various chalk tunnels arcing below the line; in the arts, the Western "I" was rediscovering its kinship with a world of Otherness still suffering under universal prejudice. On the surface of life, in waking reality, spread out all the imperialistic boundaries of race and power; underneath I and Thou, the modern legs of Hercules, were the mole courts of a great reunion of the races in the Western imagination, whose collective vision in 20th century art celebrated a vast underworld carnival where high and low, common and strange, all mingled freely and shared the same bottle. As I wound up my lecture, I could see the jots and dashes and figures on the blackboard slowly take form in their notebooks. It was moving to see such young orthodox whites patiently copy out a scheme of revolutionary principles which their own lives had not yet encountered beyond the classroom. In a small but memorable instance, my own "I" had crossed over, in the muddled way of notes on a lecture. But we had connected, finally, and without them, I doubt I would have reached the point of a simple premise on which to hang everything that follows in this little study.

In writing various versions of these chapters, I am particularly grateful for the encouragement and assistance of Clayton Eshleman himself, who graciously provided me with his private papers and unpublished manuscripts, answered my endless queries and requests for leads, but who stayed clear of my judgements and speculations. He realized early on that I was not writing so much about him as through him to the period and culture surrounding him. I also appreciate the astute criticism of Gyula Kodolanyi and Donald Pearce, who read portions of the manuscript and helped me to refine my views. Some of the ur-texts of the book were typed and criticized by my wife Catherine, whose reactions always send me back to the desk to revise and clarify my thoughts. The final manuscript was very ably prepared by Martha Casey. To my father I owe a great debt of thanks for the education I received while living abroad much of my youth; his career in the U.S. Foreign Service gave me a varied life in Lebanon, the Philippines, and pre-war Saigon, where this book was initially conceived.

The notes which begin on page 227 are keyed to the text by page number so that a reader who wishes to ignore them will not be disturbed by markers in the text itself.

KEY TO MAJOR TEXTS BY CLAYTON ESHLEMAN

MN   *Mexico & North.* Tokyo, 1962.

I   *Indiana.* Los Angeles: Black Sparrow Press, 1969

A   *Altars.* Los Angeles: Black Sparrow Press, 1971.

C   *Coils.* Los Angeles: Black Sparrow Press, 1973.

TGW   *The Gull Wall.* Los Angeles: Black Sparrow Press, 1975.

WSM   *What She Means.* Santa Barbara: Black Sparrow Press, 1978.

HM   *Hades in Manganese.* Santa Barbara: Black Sparrow Press, 1981.

F   *Fracture.* Santa Barbara: Black Sparrow Press, 1983.

NER   *The Name Encanyoned River: Selected Poems 1960–1985,* Introduction by Eliot Weinberger. Santa Barbara: Black Sparrow Press, 1986.

HCR   *Hotel Cro-Magnon.* Santa Rosa: Black Sparrow Press, 1989.

AS   *Antiphonal Swing: Selected Prose 1962–1987,* ed. Caryl Eshleman. Kingston, New York: McPherson & Co., 1989.

Minding the Underworld:
Clayton Eshleman and Late Postmodernism

Chapter One

Waves of Energy

Now, the poem not only proclaims the dynamic and necessary coexistence of opposites, but also their ultimate identity. And this reconciliation, which does not imply a reduction or transmutation of the singularity of each term, is a wall that Western thought has refused to leap over or to perforate as yet. . . . Mysticism and poetry have thus lived in a subsidiary, clandestine and diminished life. The consequences of that banishment of poetry are more evident and frightening each day: man is in exile from the cosmic flux and from himself. Because now no one is unaware that Western metaphysics ends in a solipsism.

. . . Western history can be seen as the history of an error, a going astray, in both senses of the word: in losing our way in the world we have become estranged from ourselves. We have to begin again.

Octavio *Paz*, The Bow and Lyre

Fable for Slumber

*An animal dwelt
In the body of a child.
Animal and child,
The man was wild.*

*The child asked all,
His appetite huge.
The world was small
Gave subterfuge.*

*Who failed the child
The animal struck
In a world too mild
The man was amok.*

*His hate a tooth,
His word a claw,
His anger truth
His ego law.*

*The child of love
Made man of hate,
The frustrated child
The animal ate.*

—Charles Olson

"Thank god hell is not dead in me."

(I 36)

I

The fifty-odd books of poetry, translations, essays and occasional writings of Clayton Eshleman constitute one of the extraordinary journeys into self by a contemporary poet. Not only is the canon a formidable volume of work and intellectual energy, the life map it unfolds gives us the routes taken by an American midwesterner who has spent his entire adult life fleeing the moral and esthetic limits imposed on him during childhood. If Eshleman's feud with Indiana reminds us of William Blake's own epic struggle against industrial England and the dregs of neoclassical thought, the connection is more than coincidence: Blake, Antonin Artaud and César Vallejo are all part of his saints' calendar of visionary rebels who dug deep to extricate their mental roots from the soil of conventional religion and morality nurturing their countrymen. To them we must add others whose labors went wholly into the process of escaping from a moral order they were spiritually and instinctually set against—especially Arthur Rimbaud. All of these figures Eshleman has translated with a fidelity that went far beyond mere literary meticulousness. The texts he chose to render chiefly focus on the moments in which these writers wrenched free of their bonds to an alien order of ideas. Eshleman not only wanted to bring their crises into English for other readers, but have his own voice mouth these syllables in their exact incantatory order as if to free himself as well. His poems elaborately devise his own anguished rebirth in which the adult imagination and its aroused passions are a midwife tugging his soul into consciousness. Indeed, Eshleman's liberation seems all the more difficult when we consider how thoroughly comfortable—universal—were the values he absorbed from parents, teachers, friends, community while growing up in the American heartland, Indianapolis. The regime there bore no resemblance to the corruptions of Peru or France, or to the shrill paranoia of England after the French Revolution. If anything, the alien was subtle, refined, invisible as air, ubiquitous as small brick houses and the dark, clean streets of midwestern river towns. The enemy was not out there in the menacing forms of an invading army or a secret police, but within, diffusely present in one's emotion, thought, beliefs, and gestures.

The midwest contributed to American literature its profound despair over the inadequacies of the American dream. The midlands never quite absorbed the faith necessary to leave unquestioned those high ideals of New England culture. Realism sprang up in the industrial and farm communities of Michigan, Illinois, Ohio, and Indiana—reporting back to New York magazines and book publishers all through the latter decades of the 19th century and well into our own the dark, grim, difficult struggle to live by the plow or the assembly line, the brutal terms of which eroded the credibility of Emerson's lofty notion of the uncompromising individual. The populations of the midlands had emigrated from Central Europe and brought with them the memory of economic hardships and the distrust of power that are the chief characteristics of midwestern literature. There has always been a deep gulf between the region's writers and the primly orthodox values of the merchant class in matters of religion, morality, and art. A midwestern writer's soul nearly always passed through a crisis in which youthful optimism broke down and a hard, disillusioned outlook took its place—in bleak disclosures of the way things really were. The midwest conceived not only William Dean Howells's ironic humor, but the harsh, cold tragedies of Theodore Dreiser. Midwestern writers uncovered for all to see how Anglo-American thought lost its charm or validity in these colder inland landscapes, where the cultural heritage was mixed and drew on different European traditions.

But the authority of the national culture was such that few writers dared to question the preeminence of its doctrines. The social institutions and households of nearly every community adopted Anglo-Americanism as the only philosophy governing life. Regardless of one's calling or potential, rationality was the highest good and individuality the highest virtue. Ancient bonds of community among racial and ethnic subgroups were accorded little value in the national perspective; the fulfillment of individual promise took precedence over family ties and communal bonds. Women, children, the unskilled and uneducated, those whose ethnic, racial, or religious identity fell outside Anglo-Saxon Protestantism, were assigned lower niches in the social hierarchy; power and prestige were greatest among white men, whose faculties for analysis and rational decisions were presumed to be purest in degree. The white male who repressed his other urges and desires to pursue an intellectual victory over life—as businessman or politician—was the paragon of culture, its principal hero and guiding spirit. His action was free of intuitive guesswork or lapses into sentimental obligation to others; the truly free person was a male whose hunter-like instincts were under the control of his logical faculties and his empirical intellect. And although the nation was crowded with diverse life styles and beliefs, only this one image of perfection held for all: black, brown, red alike, women, Jews, and Catholics. Until the 1950s, the U.S. and England and its immediate industrial partners of Western Europe formed a rigidly defined and organized monoculture whose members prospered or failed according to their adherence to its philosophical dictates; all outsiders were inferiors on whom it was fair, even noble, to prey for the benefit of the enlightened.

Behind America's endorsement of English ideology was the profound desire to be identified culturally and racially with the Anglo-Saxon ideal. As America's population became more and more mixed with immigrant blood from the rest of Europe and the world, the more insistent became its maintenance of English customs and beliefs; by the end of the 19th century, Anglo-Americanism had become the bedrock of social institutions and cultural life. This alliance was strengthened as the two cultures shared preeminence as industrial civilizations. The English tongue became the world's language of commerce and stood for the values and character, the staunchly practical and inventive nature of the Anglo-Saxon line. So long as its imperial machinery stood in place, England remained a powerful geopolitical force with the U.S. riding its coattails—as trading rival, military ally, and heir apparent to its global hegemony. Other Western empires followed the pattern of England's, but lacking a clear monopoly over industrial technology, they humbly took the leavings of English imperialism and developed colonies along its peripheries. Even the subtlest customs and manners in the small towns of America took their authority from the long historic successes of the British race. What gave the thrust of absolute authority to British ways was the constant reminder that its businesses and war machinery girdled the earth and held almost every other culture under its thumb. The U.S. could only follow its path and model its industries, international transactions, and foreign affairs on the example of Britain.

There were many racial and ethnic strains in American literature, but British orthodoxy ruled in matters of form and expression, and the plot of most writing showed the conquering spirit of rationality over passion, instinct, or other racial heritages. When Gatsby attempts to win Daisy's heart by imitating the Anglo-Saxon ideal, he loses his life, while the rich, Fitzgerald remarks glumly, resumed their

Anglo-Saxon privacy at the apex of the social pyramid. Gatz was a midwestern Jew, the average ethnic citizen whose only desire was to fit in with a racial and religious elite; his failure was the same seal of doom which Dreiser conferred on his own failed characters. Americans had refined their best into an untitled aristocracy whose money, religion, and racial pedigree put them beyond reach of the ethnically diverse average. The ordinary won their place in life by strict adherence to the work ethic, the principle of self-interest and its fulfillment in terms of material goods. Once into the fold, one joined the ranks of an ethnocentric enclave that ridiculed otherness and the primitive—as the remnants of pre-industrial society, the dregs of unenlightened humanity. The chosen were different, and their virtues and ideals were poured into the ears of American children the moment they entered the classroom. Against their unimpeachable rule Eshleman has raged and lyricized, while wringing changes on himself that would cast him among the ranks of Otherness in America. In 1983 he wrote ruefully in his introduction to *Fracture*: "At the moment I feel that spring may have gone out of the world," and we now "find ourselves at an odd bend in the amplitude and awfulness of life," with an "adult value system that is opposed to sex, growth, primitives and change," an "atrophy of the already severely constricted Renaissance ideals, finished and isolated bodies now pressed into the service of maintaining the status quo."

World War II shattered the British empire and the rest of Western imperial machinery crumbled soon after; the newly risen superpowers, the USSR and the U.S., were suddenly confronted with an array of new states emerging out of the ruins of the colonial world. Almost as suddenly, the world seemed overtaken by a spirit of self-determination that soon found its voice among Third World artists wishing to revive the native traditions Britain and Europe had been degrading for centuries. Self-determination required for its political and social coherence a revival of native mythology and religious beliefs, folk heroes, customs, food ways, and tribalism as the firm basis of ethnic identity—if the new states were to withstand the meddling and aggression of the U.S. and Russia in the Cold War years. African statesmen had been educated in Western universities and advocated industrialization programs requiring aid and technical assistance from their former imperial masters, a process which drove others to reassert ever more vehemently the virtues of the old ways against the modernizers and "Westernizers" of their newly independent societies. A profound consequence of the new international order was the sudden arousal of native folkways and customs in the U.S. among the very groups whose racial or ethnic heritage had been sorely abused by Anglo-Saxon prejudice. The sudden formation of a Third World of native cultures awakened the spirit of cultural diversity in the U.S. The 1950s were years of social unrest among America's minorities as they raised the very issues over civil rights that Third World nations brought to the U.N.

Postmodernism as a literary movement sprang up in response to the new geopolitical order and immediately began testing its innovations and experiments along the cracks and crevices of a faltering Anglo-American orthodoxy. In poetry, the "first heave," as Olson would say in 1950, was to replace iambic pentameter as an English-bred prosody with an organic measure drawn directly from the breath, the human body. What the imperialists had condemned as an inferior natural order would now be hailed as the redemptive sources of the new literature, an esthetic program that would center on the functions of the human organism and dwell on all those social principles that native non-Western cultures had fashioned in their arts. Anglo-Saxon ideology was put on its head to derive a Postmodern esthetic; the old icons of natural energy and folk wisdom, intuition and magic, mythology and the collective imagination were newly revered as forces to counter the role of the logical intellect and its empirical procedures, the preeminence of the individual and its ego principle, the racial arrogance of Anglo-Saxonism and its long religious heritage of abstract, i.e., disembodied, gods. Mixed with these up-endings of the social gospel were the anxieties and frustrations of a generation of World War II veteran poets who had witnessed the ravages of atomic warfare, whose disgust with the technology of slaughter turned them toward the virtues of primitive, agricultural life styles and the tribal ethics of so-called backward peoples. "White guilt" took many forms in early postmodern writing, but its main thrust was to rediscover the buried affinities between white and other races, to revamp the meaning of Otherness and circulate the term throughout discussions of literary ideology, and to confess as members of the old imperial guard one's repentance for the sins committed on behalf of Western expansion. In 1983 Eshleman summarized the aftershocks of Western imperialism thus:

> as a white Anglo-Saxon heterosexual male, I must confront the fact that what I represent as a social identity is the great boulder that must be rolled away from the entrance to the cave in which the energies of the minorities throughout the world have been sealed.
>
> (*F* 17)

And as Robert Duncan noted in his essay, "Rites of Participation," reprinted in Jerome Rothenberg's *Symposium of the Whole* (1983):

> The drama of our time is the coming of all men into one fate, "the dream of everyone, everywhere." The fate or dream is the fate of more than mankind. Our secret Adam is written now in the script of the

primal cell. We have gone beyond the reality of the incomparable nation or race, the incomparable Jehovah in the shape of a man, the incomparable Book or Vision, the incomparable species, in which identity might hold & defend its boundaries against an alien territory. All things have come now into their comparisons. But these are the correspondences that haunted Paracelsus, who saw also that the key to man's nature was hidden in the larger nature.

(327)

The anthropologist Victor Turner also observed in the *Symposium* that

becoming aware of the potency of other traditions of thought and expressive culture is itself an act of "making visible" and at the same time an entering into reflexive relations with peoples, genders, classes, ethnicities, the sick, the marginal and the troubled, all of whom from beyond the pale or beneath our bureaucratic rationality insist that we are them. Their presence and their cultural product are "metacommentaries" on our own lifeways—in which we are becoming increasingly disappointed as their lack of grace or blessing becomes more obvious.

(340)

Turner, Stanley Diamond, Dennis Tedlock and scores of other writers in Rothenberg's *Symposium* felt that Western civilization's overweening attitude to the rest of the world was reflected in its ethnocentricity, its plundering of natural resources, and its disregard for other cultures and social systems. The arts had likewise become rigidly circumscribed by a preeminent concern for the autonomy of the individual, an ideology which ignored the group mind, tradition, folk lore, the nature wisdom of the past. The job of ethnopoetics for Gary Snyder is to combat the West's "unparalleled waterfall of destruction of a diversity of human cultures; plant species; animal species; of the richness of the biosphere and the millions of years of organic evolution that have gone into it. In a sense ethnopoetics is like some field of zoology which is studying disappearing species." Those "four thousand different languages and cultures [are] being swept away in the inexorable push towards monoculture."

Hence, Olson's anatomy of Ahab in *Call Me Ishmael* (1947) as the essential Western hero, the refined, granitic ego answerable only to self and the tyrant over that microcosm of the Third World, his crew. The turning point in Western civilization, Turner believes, was the collapse of its empires at the mid-20th century, and the emergence out of colonial obscurity of still vital, largely coherent native cultures which began voicing their complex identities in world forums. Truman's Point Four Program, the U.S. State Department's Agency for International Development, and countless new trade alliances between the U.S. and remote, foreign cultures confronted America with a world of cultural plurality, a "hall of mirrors" whose "therapeutic function," in Turner's words, was to confront Westerners with "the problem of the One and the Many—a new reflexivity in itself" (341).

How Eshleman handles these issues is the point of this book. His approach is at once more personal and more diffuse thematically. His models for the poems are not to be found in the American poetic tradition, at least not directly. His main influences are taken from South American, Spanish and French literature; and within these cultures, it is the outraged and diffident voices pitted against authority, government censorship, the weight of traditional (repressive) society that form his elected heritage. Eshleman's battle is with himself and the midwestern culture that formed him. His poetry is the arena in which he takes on his oppressors and the self he was given by his elders; what usually transpires in his lyric frames is a violent debate, an eruption of dense speech that moves like emotional lava out of some area of blocked awareness, as he finds the weaknesses in his opponent's argument or locates the loose brick in the walls he tells us run all through his mind.

The poems are not constructs of ideological alternatives, as they are in the work of Gary Snyder or Robert Kelly, where a pastoral or pagan ideal is elaborated; Eshleman assumes we know what the new ideals are, and takes himself to task for having nourished some contrary notion or been slow in changing his ways and attitudes. He blames his region and parents for making him into a conventional male, giving him the daunting task of reconstituting himself emotionally and psychologically, which he makes the principal drama of his writing. Eshleman's sense of the poem is that it must grapple with the state of one's self, the wounded, ailing, or culpable self and subject it to a kind of dialogical court in which it is accused, sentenced, and repents in a lush torrent of surreal eloquence. The plot unfolding in his prolific canon is of a man moving inexorably toward the goal of renewal, of self-transformation from what he was made, hammered into on his regional anvil, to what he desires to be: a liberated, balanced, enriched man, given deeper sensitivity to the plight of others, with "light" darkened by his feminine reserves of psyche, and turned outward to the world. Or, as he puts it later in his work, he is a man destroying the "House of Eshleman" and moving on to become a guest at the Hotel Cro-Magnon, the hotel of human dreams, whose basement reaches into the underworld, and whose rooms are occupied by all who have lived and dealt with their tragic human natures.

Eshleman's poetic vision is of the one *becoming* the many through a kind of penitential lyricism, in which the darker, guiltier poetries of the Catholic world assist him in the sometimes gruesome rituals of transformation, which take us all the way from hypothetical suicides by means of Japanese evisceration or *seppuku,* to odyssean orbits around the zodiac, and finally, through love, meditation, and the suspenseful treks he makes through the caves of southwestern France. His unique journey toward love takes him back to the ground of his childhood and from there into manhood, his marriages, his struggles to become a poet, his ordeal at midlife with the last resistant forces of his old, conventional self. There is no end to the roots to be pulled up in order to declare a new self. Indeed, if Pound said to poets to "make it new," Eshleman responds with a poetry that makes new the self, from which comes a new poetry of compassion and vision. That process of rebirth is both bloody and violent, and occasionally self-indulgent in its histrionics, but it is work that captures the essence of Postmodern angst and the ideals driving literary experiment toward the pole of dreams and ecstatic encounters with the soul.

Technically, Eshleman's poems are variations on blank verse; many of his lines scan to approximately ten syllables or enjamb in units of eleven or twelve syllables marked off by commas or line breaks, as they move forward at the pace of conversation. The *mise en page* is Olson's; the layouts are projective and yet not—typically, Eshleman's lines enjamb to keep the eye moving, to prevent end-stopping unless he is terminating a sentence. The layouts are not, as in Olson's early poetry, maps of intellection or scores for the speaking voice; the line structures are intended, I think, to distribute an orthodox metrical scheme over open ground, to liberate the lines as much as possible while ordering them from within by a partially concealed iambic tempo.

> How clean, transparent and opaque
> Our father of the Caves is, at St.-Cirq

begins "The Decanting" (*HM* 106–08) followed almost at once by a deformation of the metric,

> How potential, how unfilled out,
> a blank interior in which my eyes
> can explore their rock, and not in black

> painted but in unlit recesses where a wave I,
> a tentacle man shaped by a dream breaker,
> starts toward paradise, . . .

As the sentence grows it flattens the blank verse into racing prose, but at a certain point Eshleman will rein in the slack of a paragraph by a blunt, sharp phrase, an interjection of short, syncopated speech, or an abrupt intrusion of surrealist imagery. Note how "The Decanting" proceeds in the next paragraph (106):

> How evil He seems in urban light, set
> like a pusher between the predictable,
> if filthy, buildings. No snake will
> flash from his unwashed skin. No jungle
> to surprise me. No spooked me to bind
> with a thousand taboos. Only one taboo:
> *you must not imagine a justifying being.*

Running like broken cord through this language is the ghost of blank verse, truncated, indeterminate, half-buried, but there as the organizing principle of the lines:

> How *e*vil He seems in *ur*ban *light, set*
> like a *push*er . . .

Its function is to provide unity *and* a dramatic voice as he heaves words accusingly at his listener. Add to this the duality of his language, a diction fusing mundane recollections to supercharged surrealist lyricism, and we have something of the composite nature of his lyric mode.

Such a style of poem slips through the main categories of American poetry; it draws on Anglo-American tradition as well as European and South American poetry. Its line is neither plain nor wholly figurative, but something inbetween, vibrating between two epistemological worlds of language. Eshleman's lyricism is a study of approximations, mergings between his Americanness as a writer and the literatures outside English he has made his principal subject as translator and critic. Where others of his generation adapted Pound's "song" or Williams' triadic stanza, or the tight trochaic clusters of Oppen and Zukofsky, Eshleman grafted a variety of open forms from Vallejo, Césaire, Rimbaud, and Artaud onto the loosely controlled base of Elizabethan dramatic verse. By such means his poems convey a strong sense of character, an individual in rigorous outline, but whose tormented interiors stand for the dissolving boundaries of modern subjectivity. An excerpt from a work-in-progress, entitled "Under World Arrest," illustrates some of the principles of his style. Notable here is the fluidity of the form—loosely phrased strophes followed by a sudden tightening of the lines as images take over—and an argumentative process which starts out with a literal situation that turns into metaphor, to the mythological landscape of allegory where a soul-voice speaks to us beyond sexual category, the voice Postmodern literature as a whole has struggled to bring to thought:

> The one who took my hand when I was very little,
>   now closing me, like an account,
> explains that after him the tabulability of things ends.
> As compensation, he has painted my eyes
>   with secularity,
>   hung zeros from my lips.
>
> He has not forgotten that by thrusting an urn of blazing
>   semen into the female dark
> we not only blackened the walls of nature,
> but turned the human heart into BC   AD,
>   two rubble arms on each side of a pit,
>   reaching
>   around the pit,
>   without bodies,
>   trying to embrace . . .

> It was crucial to see that my face in water
> an image of my face
> is neither mother nor father
> but a shadow into whose interior
> fish can pass, investing Narcissus
> with passing otherness
> as this phantom ripples apart.
>
> If I am hooped over history, a mockery of Isis,
> it is because, with my fingers in Lascaux
> and my toes scraping the present,
> I have sought unbearable images for an age
> whose concreteness is mixed with those
> who were commanded from the ramps.

Eshleman's lush, frequently overwrought language, laid on with a palette knife, is a consequence of the mixing of disparate cultures in his style. The realism of daily life is his English root, the Protestant angle of his esthetic; we know these are details and not images, and take them as the literal signs of experience. When they explode into lyric grotesques, Catholic Europe is breaking into his monolog, depositing Pound's world into his language: the realm of Pan, the libidinous world of transformation from animal and plant to human and back again. Eshleman's language does not try to maintain both traditions but rather juxtaposes them in the same lyric so as to subvert the one, the literal Protestant vision of life as struggle for self-control, by the other, the self-dissolving forces of Otherness gleaned from Catholic and pagan art.

When postmodernism sprang up at the collapse of European and British empires at mid-century, it was, in Rothenberg's phrase, "a desire for a new beginning . . . a return of what Blake called 'our antediluvian energies,' " or what Michael McClure described as "a *massive* return to 'instinct and intuition.' " Olson asked the main question to poets in "The Kingfishers" (1949): what could be gained by believing the "other" side, the native cultures at home and among the ex-colonies of the new age?

> I pose you your question:
> Shall you uncover honey where maggots are?
> I hunt among stones

But for a time after the publication of Donald Allen's *The New American Poetry 1945–1960* (1960), Postmodern writing seemed to recede behind the tumultuous public events of the "hippie" years, a second wave of responses to the end of the imperialist age when youths wore the symbols and costumes of so-called primitive people, formed communes and practiced basic crafts and rudimentary agriculture, adopted native customs and religions, or found expression through the ritualistic performances of rock groups—an era culminating in the Woodstock festival and the protest marches and riots that broke out in 1968 from Mexico to Berkeley, Chicago and Paris—as youths rebelled against the policies of the old order. The 1960s marked the point at which youths had discovered their political power. The mystique of the group or tribe had come to stand for an alternative ideological principle. Not only had "group-therapy" become a popular form of rehabilitation for the beleaguered individuals of mass society, others even applied the value of group identity to corporate structure, as in Eric Berne's *The Structure and Dynamics of Organizations and Groups* (1963), an effort at contriving a kind of ethnocapitalist alternative.

But Postmodern writing continued evolving in the work of a small group of poets in New York who identified their writing as "deep image" poetry. Jerome Rothenberg, Robert Kelly, David Antin, Armand Schwerner, Rochelle Owens, and George Economou, all (but Schwerner, who attended Columbia) graduates of the City College of New York, made up the core of the group. Diane Wakoski, from California, joined them in 1960; Eshleman had learned of the group from another CCNY graduate, Jack Hirschman, and began publishing poems in *Trobar*, founded by Kelly and Economou in 1960. For Rothenberg, who had grown up in the Jewish ghettoes of Manhattan's lower east side and the south Bronx, and Kelly, raised in Catholic neighborhoods in Brooklyn, New York was Whitman's cosmos of gathered races and religions. They wanted poetry to express its diversity of cultural attitudes, and draw together the extremes of its religious life. A century after Whitman's debut, poets were still trying to break up Anglo-Americanism by means of New York's pluralism.

Rothenberg coined the term "deep image" in a prose-poem that appeared in the journal *Poems from the Floating World*, published in 1960 by his own Hawk's Well Press.

> From deep within us it comes: the
>   wind that moves through the lost
>   branches, hurts us with a wet cry,
>   as if an ocean were caged in each skull:
>
> There is a sea of connection that floats
>   between men: a place where speech
>   is touch and the welcoming hand
>   restores its silence: an ocean
>   warmed by dark suns.
>
> The deep image rises from the shoreless
>   gulf: here the poet reaches down
>   among the lost branches, till a
>   moment of seeing: the poem. Only
>   then does the floating world sink again
>   into its darkness, leaving a white
>   shadow, and the joy of our having been
>   here, together.

In the late 1950s, Rothenberg and Kelly began reexploring Pound's Imagism for a way around the verse orthodoxy inspired by New Criticism back to the roots of Modernist experiment. Though not a movement in the formal sense, "deep image" poetry introduced Jungian archetypal psychology into poetry, the most significant innovation to be wrung on Pound's Image since the objectivist movement of the 1930s. Rothenberg, Kelly and others of the group began using archetypal images as the means for generating commentaries, arguments, recollections that led away from self toward the opposite pole of awareness, the "other."

The "deep image" implied there is a hidden source of being and ideas within selfhood that had been driven underground to the irrational depths of mind, whose kinship is primitive society, ancient nature religions, perhaps even the primordial beginnings of human life itself. This is the part of self that had become alienated from other mental functions in modern life; its absence in thought was part of the sickness of contemporary culture. In an "Editorial" printed in the opening issue of *Trobar* (1960), the editors Economou, Robert and Joan Kelly announced their intentions as follows:

> Poetry is itself a power of life. The editors of *Trobar* believe that American poetry today must reestablish contact with the perennial strength of the deep image as a mode of working within the poem, as statement and as vision.

The archetypal imagination is a window onto nature and the continuities of life beyond individuality, according to these poets. Without its voice in thought, the self is dominated by the rapacious ego, whose drive to power overwhelms the other impulses of self leading to community. Modern society was composed of isolated selves ruled by rationality and egoism, the fear of death, which had led to imperialist drives to power over so-called primitive societies, the "other" humanity of Africa, Asia, Australia, Oceania, Indian America. "Deep image" poetry was, from the start, a therapeutic art, a use of archetypal psychology to plumb depths of imagination to restore this underworld to self, and thus recover the healthy, balanced psyche.

Writing in *Trobar* 3 (1961), Rothenberg answered the question "Why *Deep* Image?" by noting that

> The power of the deep image is its ability to convey a
> sense of two-worlds-in-one: directly: with no concept
> to come between the inner experience and its mean-
> ing. With this comes a new attack on the mystery of
> the real, in which all our habitual perceptions are con-
> tinually being put in question. The poet discovers the
> unknown by creating it from the vast resources of his
> inner life, the savings of an experienced world still rich
> in meaning: he delivers, as deep image, the life-giving
> vision that he could in no other way explain.

Looking back in 1968, Kelly wrote in *Statement,* a brochure commemorating the "deep image" group, "it was our thought to get blood-life back in the *line*"

> wch is syntax & history
> & beast-desire, when since the 20s we have been assailed
> day & night by noise, false or suspect informations,
> caressive syntax in all media, & all men have shut down,
> banked cortical measures against the blast of words
>
> & we had to get through, the line, the hypersyntactic,
> the silence, to disturb the normal deadening flow, the
> line, life/line, to get thru to your ears rightly
> stuffed against madness
>   how to reach you

Though "deep image" was an ephemeral movement, perhaps only a splinter from Black Mountain and Beat poetry, it nonetheless had a structure, a publishing network. A book cooperative had been set up on East 10th Street dubbed by Kelly "The Blue Yak" (after a poem by Gregory Corso, "The Mad Yak" in *Gasoline,* 1958), where Hawk's Well books, publications of Jargon, Origin Press, Totem, Corinth, other alternative presses, the magazines *Yugen, Trobar, Origin* were on display if rarely sold; readings were held at local coffeehouses and at the newly formed YMHA Poetry Center; occasionally music and poetry came together (Rothenberg and Kelly once put together an evening of medieval lyrics and jazz). Wakoski's companion in 1960, the avant-garde composer Lamont Young, staged concerts (proto-"happenings") at Yoko Ono's loft on Chambers Street in lower Manhattan, where Wakoski took the tickets. Young's interest in John Cage gave Wakoski exposure to the other arts, which in turn she introduced to Rothenberg and friends. Other poets came around, including Jackson Mac Low, later an important influence on David Antin and Armand Schwerner; Robert Bly and W. S. Merwin, both living in New York at the time, came into the movement and brought it to prominence in the mid-1960s.

"Deep image" poetry had plumbed the "other" imagination in modern American writing, invented, fleshed out a second, hidden personality of poetry—a wilderness interior of mind or sensibility. This was the illicit natural self, the inner life of the soul, concealed behind conventionality and cautious living in the censorious 1950s. Thinking back on these years, Wakoski now recalls the double life of women especially—their roles as providers for their lovers and husbands. Their uniform—stockings, high heels, blouse and skirt—was put on each morning to go to work—Diane Rothenberg to a junior high school, Wakoski to the British Book Center uptown; their men wrote, composed, hustled the lean opportunities of those years. Landlords pried into the nature of relationships; one hid the truth from conventional society much of the time, disguising, prevaricating, misleading—while exploring another life in the arts, on the bohemian fringe. Evenings were spent at the San Remo bar in the Village or at the Cedar Tavern, or at loft "rent parties," when there was money to buy a drink or gain entrance.

By the summer of 1961, some of the group began to disperse. The Rothenbergs left for Europe, Kelly went to Bard College in upstate New York to teach, Eshleman went to Taiwan, and the Blue Yak closed its doors for good. New York itself was undergoing deep changes—it was the end of an era as pop art replaced abstract expressionism in the galleries, and the hippies took over the "scene" in the Village. But there were bonds among the members that kept their poetry alive if not the movement. In 1964, Rothenberg and Kelly collaborated on a short book, *Sightings and Lunes* (Hawk's Well Press), in which the short poem was pushed to new limits. Rothenberg opens *Sightings* with his original "deep image" prose-poem; in Kelly's *Lunes,* the lune is an imagist précis, a momentary lyric in which a deep image is suspended, like a moonbeam. By then, the group had published first and second books, and matured to the point that movements were no longer important. In Kelly's words in the *Statement* of 1968, "We've vanished into our lives of work, & I see them seldom, perhaps they see themselves seldom, we all have new friends too & different places & lives elsewhere, & that makes all the difference in personal history, in the making of americans."

By the mid-1960s Rothenberg turned his interest toward other cultures through translations and his earliest anthologies—*Ritual* (1966) and *Technicians of the Sacred* (1967, 1985), and in poems about his own situation as a Jew in America whose ancestry went back to the pogroms of Poland and beyond to a history of religious/racial persecution that was his own heritage as a member of a minority. The deep image was now to be found among these other cultural and racial groups, the voice of a collective imagination which emanated from the discourse of rites, ceremonies, myth narratives, chants. The deep image was thus a natural mode of speech for those who had not purged the functions of the unconscious from their waking lives. Western poets struggled to hear this voice and urged others to believe it was the underlying unconscious that spoke its dreams in poetry.

The search for its natural use in other cultures meant that Westerners hungry for spiritual answers would poke their noses into the private integrity of these other societies and once more exploit their resources for imperial ends. "We come in with our analytical minds & shatter the unity [of aboriginal societies], which has in fact been shattered already by workers before us," Rothenberg wrote. He was convinced that what existed as the folkways and arts of primal society was at the base of 20th century experimental art—the source it groped toward in its endless ruminations over openness, spontaneity, the powers of image and chant, randomness and repetition. In primal poetry, "forms are often open," he argued, "causality is often set aside." "The poet (who may be dancer, singer, magician, whatever the event demands of him) masters a series of techniques that can fuse the most seemingly contradictory propositions." This way Dada itself had tended, as had the whole phalanx of movements we call postmodern art. Primitive expression had all along been the aim of 20th century expression, as each movement stripped off a layer of egocentric modality and plunged deeper toward selflessness, into the realm of collective dreaming. "A poetry of the spirit—a visionary poetry—is not only to be found apart from us," he wrote in the 1985 edition of *Technicians*; "while it pervades many old cultures, it has, since the nineteenth century at least, been a prominent mode among our own poets

(& in some sense has likely always been that, as a kind of crypto [hidden] vision."

Technicians of the Sacred captured the spirit of the 1960s in its search for cultural alternatives. The source of vision lay all along in the subjugated cultures of the old imperial order, under the very noses of the masters. The real gold of the jungles was not buried deep in the mountains but in the minds, customs, bonds of tribal life itself. As the West grew brittle and obsessive within the boundaries of its monoculture, the societies along its peripheries were rich in the resources of healthy human nature. Its ways were food for the Western soul, but so far only poets and ethnographers seemed aware of this fact. The soul atrophied in rationality and consciousness; the dark was the soul's medium, which primal life incorporated into thought. "Primitive," Snyder wrote in his essay, "The Politics of Ethnopoetics," "is not a word that means past, but *primary*, and *future*." Primitive describes the orders of thought by which one possesses knowledge "in community with the other people—non-human included—brothers and sisters." A poetry of individual mind is merely one "line of thinking in the West," an Athenian poetics which should not stand for all that has occurred in occidental art. By careful discriminations, one can expose the primitive origins of European ethnicity, as Rothenberg sets out to do in his revised edition of *Technicians,* and further isolate the Athenian branch of abstract reason that set in motion Western monocultural drift. In Snyder's view, "An expansionist imperialist culture feels most comfortable when it is able to believe that the people it is exploiting are somehow less than human. When it begins to get some kind of feedback that these people might be human beings like themselves it becomes increasingly difficult" (*The Old Ways* 30).

Otherness in the postmodern view includes the body, the physical sources of awareness, as well as alien cultures and modes of existence. Imperialism not only split the geopolitical scheme of nations but the sensibility of the imperators as well—a split between "lower" and "higher" functions, genital and mental centers of awareness. "We," i.e., American whites, Rothenberg says in his preface to *Shaking the Pumpkin,* "will never be whole without a recovery of the 'red [Amerindian] power' that's been here from the beginning. The true integration must begin & end with a recognition of all such powers . . . we're doomed without his tribal and matrilocal wisdom, which can be shared only among equals who have recognized a common lineage from the earth" (xix). Ethnopoetics is not only a poetic but a therapy. In the companion to *Technicians,* the ethnological essays in *Symposium of the Whole,* the Rothenbergs, Jerome and Diane, bring science and the humanities into the widening perspective on the "primitive." Only one selection draws on the old '30s critique of imperialism from the left, a passage from the "Communist Manifesto" on the evils of the managerial class. An "ethnopoetics" surfaces in both of Rothenberg's anthologies as he brings together various critiques of the imperial enemy. Alongside Olson's "Human Universe" in *Symposium* you will find Aimé Césaire's bitter treatise "On Negritude."

But as Rothenberg quickly points out in the "Pre-face" to *Symposium,* "The present gathering will center on the poetics of the matter," the revival of interest in so-called "savage" cultures, and avoid the overt political debate on the conduct, morality, consequences of four centuries of Western expansion. "*Ethno*poetics" as Rothenberg describes it is "the attempt to define a primary human potential." The value of rediscovering other cultures lay in overcoming "a mindless mechanization that has run past any uses it may once have had." The anthology is a kind of herbal medicine, for these texts have long been missing from the Western intellectual diet. "In such a new 'totality,' " Rothenberg quotes

Duncan, " 'all the old excluded orders must be included.' "
Duncan's list is a roll call of targets and issues in post-WWII
social reform: "The female, the proletariat, the foreign; the
animal and vegetative; the unconscious and the unknown;
the criminal and failure—all that has been outcast and vaga-
bond must return to be admitted in the creation of what we
consider we are." Here then are the healing powers of
animacy, magic, charms, spells, incantations, visions, dreams
and fantasies driven from thought in the philosophical
upheavals of European reform. Consider this Navajo song
from Rothenberg's North American Indian anthology, *Shaking the Pumpkin:*

> THEREFORE I MUST TELL THE TRUTH
>
> I am ashamed before the earth:
> I am ashamed before the heavens:
> I am ashamed before the dawn:
> I am ashamed before the evening twilight:
> I am ashamed before the blue sky:
> I am ashamed before the darkness:
> I am ashamed before the sun:
> *I am ashamed before that standing within
>   me which speaks with me.*
>
> Some of these things are always looking at me.
> I am never out of sight.
> Therefore I must tell the truth.
> That is why I always tell the truth.
> *I hold my word tight to my breast.*
>
> (*Pumpkin* 11)

It is Rothenberg's task to show that the "they" of his equa-
tion is not strange or antithetical, but a neglected portion of
the Westerner's own soul—the dark Other degraded as witch-
craft, cannibalism, unevolved or retrograde mental states.

A confrontation with the other has been a slow process, but Rothenberg's preface to *Shaking the Pumpkin* pinpoints the post-WWII era as a new start at understanding its values, *uses* to a fractious Western perspective:

> The difference in our own time was to smash that imperial and swollen mold to shift the primary scene from Greece, say, to the barbaric or paleolithic part, or to the larger, often still existing tribal world, and to see in that world (however "outcast and vagabond" it had been made to look) a complexity of act and vision practiced by proto-poets/proto-artists who were true "technicians of the sacred." And along with this shift came the invention and revival of *specific* means: new materials and instruments (plastic and neon, film and tape) alongside old or foreign ones (stones, bones, and skin; drums, didjeridoos, and gamelans); ancient roles and modes of thought that had survived at the Western margins (sacred clowns and dancers, shamanistic ecstasies, old and new works of dream and chance); but, as Victor Turner describes it, "an immense orchestration of genres in all available sensory codes: Speech, music, singing; the presentation of elaborately worked objects, such as masks; wall-paintings, body-paintings; sculptured forms; complex, many-tiered shrines; costumes; dance forms with complex grammars and vocabularies of bodily movements, gestures, and facial expressions."

Contemporary poets are the "defenders of an endangered human diversity" linking up with those figures outside the "great tradition" who represented that "diversity . . . and many of the values being uncovered in the new poetic enterprises." The word "recover" is used often in this preface, as elsewhere in ethnopoetic writing with unwitting insistence on the medicinal value of unlocking the body through the "reemergence of suppressed and rejected forms and images (the goddess, the trickster, the human universe, etc.)" The thesis emerges that racism springs from the opposed self, that war between mind and body epically expanded into vast ethnocentric movements of empires. The West, by implication, is a patient under care of its "marginal" artist/healers, whose rediscoveries of once maligned and dismissed human counterparts lead the way back to wholeness and well-being.

Technicians and *Symposium of the Whole,* with their companion anthologies by Allen, *The New American Poetry* and *The Poetics of the New American Poetry,* take up a half-foot on the library shelf but enclose a mid-century debate on poetry and the imperial heritage: Anglo-American tradition versus a range of alien literature coming into Western consciousness. In none of them will you find defenders of the old Anglo alliance. These are outsider anthologies whose figures were until recently left out of the standard textbooks students lug to literary survey classes throughout the U.S. In the *Symposium,* the Rothenbergs seized the opportunity to legitimize an alternative body of writing; their book is an "intersection between poetry and anthropology," with sober field studies by Bronislaw Manlinowski, Paul Radin, Ruth Finnegan, Stanley Diamond, Ramon Medina Silva corroborating the speculations of the poets. In the *Symposium* one finds Clayton Eshleman grappling with paleolithic ghosts in the company of Roland Barthes "reading" the painted faces of Noh and Kabuki actors, or Snyder and Alfonso Ortiz both appreciating the archetypal complexity of trickster/clown figures. In "Contemporary Moves," the closing section of the *Symposium,* a host of poets mixes with social scientists, their races, sexes and cultures finding a point of convergence in their collective interest in, say, the irrational dimensions of art.

II

This was the cultural ferment in which Eshleman first began writing poems. In 1959, Eshleman enrolled in the graduate literature program at Indiana University, where he began a friendship with Jack Hirschman, a poet and student in comparative literature who had organized a reading series of European and Latin American poetry he called the "Babel" readings. From the start of his career, Eshleman pursued literature from sources outside the realm of English, along its peripheries in France, Spain, in hispanic Central and South America. In the summers of 1958 and 1959, he made his pilgrimage to Mexico, where he labored over preliminary translations of Pablo Neruda's poems, later drafts of which appeared as *Residence on Earth*, published in San Francisco in 1962, and wrote some of the poems of his first book, *Mexico & North*, which he published himself in Tokyo in 1962. Mexico and Japan constituted two of the important "centers" of Postmodern activity in the non-English world, strongholds of Catholicism and Buddhism.

At Indiana, Eshleman gravitated to the English Department's literary review, *Folio*, a tri-quarterly which had been languishing after a previous student-editor had mishandled several of its issues. When Eshleman, who had been the assistant editor, offered to take control of the journal, a faculty advisor gave him the editorship and *Folio* was successfully revived. In three issues, Eshleman filled its pages with a gallery of foreign poets in translation and some of the leading figures of American Postmodernism: Zukofsky, Duncan, Ginsberg, Creeley, and Corso. Already Eshleman was participating in the groundswell of resistance to British culture abroad and at home, deftly gathering his own body of diverse writings into an orchestrated alternative cultural push. His cues were coming directly from *Black Mountain Review, Kulchur, Origin, Yugen, Trobar,* and other organs of the avant-garde. But after only three issues, publication of *Folio* was ended for good; Eshleman had been censored for publishing poems by Ginsberg and Zukofsky!

1960 was a beginning of change in the American midlands; though *Folio* was finished, Eshleman had made contact with writers in New York through Hirschman and a sympathetic friend, Mary Ellen Solt, then a housewife married to a history professor at Indiana, Leo Solt. Her contact with Williams led Eshleman to Cid Corman, a crucial figure in the Black Mountain movement and publisher of *Origin.* New York was a frenzy of art movements either reaching their peak or already beginning to fade away, just as Eshleman was introducing himself. By 1958 or so, there were two currents of literature in the city: the influences of European surrealism brought over by war-time emigrés and finding new uses in American writing, and a purely native tradition of experiment with myth, projective forms, improvisational modes stimulated by Olson and his circle at Black Mountain.

Eshleman's entrée into New York publishing was through the deep imagists, to whom he began sending Neruda translations and some of his first attempts at surrealist writing. Though his poem "Roaches" was published in *Trobar,* Rothenberg and Kelly both had reservations about the autobiographical emphasis of Eshleman's poetry. The deep image was an impersonal figure dredged from below personal history, or so it seemed. What Eshleman tried to show was the damaged psyche living under its manufactured identity; his poetry was a narrative of the psyche as victim, the ailing spirit that heals itself by examining its agonizing memories and sorting out its feelings. Eshleman wanted poetry to heal emotional, spiritual injury, a facet of the deep image only Wakoski had so far explored. Eshleman's analysis of his own life exposed a sensitive youth reared on bourgeois values and provincial sterility. The transformation of that self became his central drama. Eshleman's rebellion against Indianapolis, recorded in *Indiana* (1969), caught the national ferment of the arts as a generation looked for the native roots of American identity.

After Eshleman arrived in Kyoto in 1962, he applied himself to the rigorous stylistic austerity of Corman's poetry, with its precision, fluidity, and close attention to sound. But Eshleman wanted to construct a lyrical model of interrupted, sidetracked thought, a lyricism that would disrupt its own narrative or thematic development with troubled memories or sudden passion and resentment. Poetry should capture the mind in the coils of its emotional debates, as reasoning gave in to rage, or grief, or fragments of recollection. Corman's poetry built models of a brief, flawless attention of mind to its own musings; but Eshleman wanted to create the structure of a volatile mental drama in which impacted or suppressed emotional content would sweep across the lyric surface and change the flow of thought. Eshleman wanted to write a poem whose edges were recognizable as lyric discourse, but whose middle dropped away and revealed a honeycomb of chaotic and rejected events, feelings, traumas, and resentments seething behind the appearance of a logical structure of thought. At the center of the poem, the psyche should transform itself by adding to its awareness from what lay underneath, in the hidden recesses of the unconscious: "In the heart of the poem there was / no longer a hesitation before / power," he wrote in his best early poem of the Kyoto years, "The Book of Yorunomado." In "The White Tiger," also from *Indiana,* he repeats this central tenet: "the imagination rejects even the most / filthy matter to its peril." Everyone possessed his own hell of suppressed mental events, a depth of psyche which selfhood excluded. It was over that mental abyss that Eshleman wanted to expose the ego, to subject it to the most abhorrent thought and experience. Anything less than a direct confrontation of one's own rejected depths led to an artificiality of response in art; and already Eshleman had begun to feel that the American tradition was fraught with compromises and evasions of the truth of human nature. The crux of his position was that the Anglo-American esthetic tradition had diminished the possibility of a descent into one's interiors to discover the areas walled up and rejected as the non-self, the Other.

In a review of William Bronk's *Life Supports: New and Selected Poems,* written in 1981, Eshleman praised the poetry as "utterly compelling, harrowing, and masterfully written," calling Bronk "the first American poet to fully engage a sense of art that is shadowed by a pervasive sense of invalidness, of inadequacy, and even failure": "His poetry is all about those things of which we have concepts but which we find non-existent or unapproachable." Bronk's prose (*The New World*) and poetry recognized the irreality of human awareness, its codified and arbitrary structure of the world, beyond which extends a nameless and undefined actuality of things ignored by a philosophically abstract self. Bronk had located the opaque membrane between concepts and the unarticulated expanse of nature, inner and outer, which has no participation in thought. Bronk measured the problem in art, even if he didn't solve it. At the other extreme were those academic poets who, like Elizabeth Bishop, made a virtue of ignoring the life unformulated by culture. Her poetry, Eshleman noted, "is on the scrupulous, completed thing, cleansed, as it were, of all the *scoriae* of birth and development. . . . and while very well written, reflects the absence of the 'other,' in any credible personal, historical or political sense." Behind the inhibitions of poetry lay deeper, more pervasive inhibitions of the American psyche, restraints and fears first imposed on its sensibility in the theological upheavals of the European Reformation, when the self was reshaped as a secular, demystified function of Protestant theology.

In Kyoto, the study of American poetry gave way to an absorption with the Peruvian poet César Vallejo, whose anguished lyricism bore all the volatility and distortion Eshleman wished to master in his own poetry. Here was a torment and disruption of thought that addressed the existence of violent undercurrents of psyche struggling to break through. The Protestant mind had sealed up the passageways of this mental abyss, perhaps by channeling all dread and anxiety into humanist aspiration, fulfillments in the social sphere. The Catholic world of Romance language cultures preserved a sense of the horrific past which made both damnation and the presence of spirit palpable realities in the world. Vallejo was the gateway to a tradition of poetry which the preëminence of English literature and culture had long ago eclipsed. The "dual natures" of the poet, Eshleman observes in *A Study of Poetic Apprenticeship,* battle for sovereignty in the act of composition. This is the war of religion fought each time an American writes a poem and struggles between knowledge and intuition, fact and mystery.

> Daemonization (in contrast to demonization) is the admitting of unconscious material into the composition-in-process, the point at which the poet weds himself, consciousness and unconsciousness fuse—the poet is the world, no separation between his skin and everything else. The eagle of inspiration has sunk its talons into the poet's shoulders and he is borne aloft. . . . Garcia Lorca, weary of hearing critics and conventional poets prattle about the Muse and the angel, borrowed from the world of Flamenco dancing the figure of the "duende," which translates into English rather poorly as "imp."

Though it would take sixteen years to transform a translation of Vallejo into a personal, American lyricism, his own poetry grew out of the protracted revisions and recasting of the final translated text. Translating Vallejo's poetry proved an essential preparation for his own writing; in 1979, when Eshleman received the National Book Award for his Vallejo book, it was also a recognition of one stage of an extensive, interrelated body of work that directed its arguments at a core of human nature which had not been adequately expressed in American poetry before.

In producing a body of work rooted in psychological concerns, Eshleman was at the front lines of a widely scattered advance to Latin American and European poetry which contained hints and glimmers of an opposite epistemological perspective. This other perspective was the attraction of French and Spanish surrealism, in whose linguistic distortions one could read the psychological upheavals of recent European history. The American political process had remained stable throughout the Depression and war years, and American writers chafed against a narrowly provincial literary tradition, which Pound had frequently denounced as sterile from his vantage point in Europe. American victory at the close of war had unleashed an unexpected reaction of sympathy, compassion, immersion in the literature of defeated powers, and of rejected cultures in Central and South America. Defeat and rejection seemed to confer a purity of exile from the Anglo-American vortex. But an even more systemic "otherness" could be found among the cultures once belonging to the Holy Roman Empire or to the Spanish Empire, whose traditions had absorbed the Catholic interests in iconography, vision, apparitions, visitations, miracles, the ritual of transubstantiation and other mythological elements outside empirical thought.

Pound's departure from England in 1920 led to a series of residences in Catholic nations; though he rejected Catholicism as a faith, he was profoundly attracted to the religion as a focus of centuries of esthetic elaboration, from Cavalcanti to Provençal literature, and to the presence of Greek and Roman paganism in its most sacred conceptions. The writers of England and the U.S. who migrated to Catholic cultures in the 20th century constitute a significant diaspora of Protestant artists who turned against the values and attitudes of their own religion; the migrations to Mexico included numerous figures of the London-Paris Modernist ferment, as Taxco and Mexico City became salon-cultures in the decade following the revolution of 1910. After World War II, Mexico was again a focus of American writing, for Williams and Stevens, then for Olson, Ginsberg, Burroughs, Kerouac, and Eshleman. Southern France and Mallorca had attracted Creeley, Blackburn, and (briefly) Robert Duncan, and other postmodern poets. For a time in the 1950s, important journals of the movement were appearing from Mexico City to Palma de Mallorca, from Paris to Kyoto.

Eshleman left Kyoto in 1964 and proceeded to Lima, Peru shortly after, where he observed first-hand the extent to which Catholicism penetrated Peruvian life and customs. In his introduction to *On Mules Sent from Chavin* (1977), he seems almost baffled by the weight of theology pressing down upon the landscape. The journal he wrote during his sojourn in Peru is a parallel commentary on native Indian culture and his own thoughts on poetry and poetics. Like Olson's *Mayan Letters* and the notebooks Ginsberg kept during his stay at Palenque in the early 1950s, Eshleman's journal combs the intricacies of an unfamiliar culture for hints of an opposing awareness. But the experience proved an intractable mystery: a suspicious and half-mad widow resisting Eshleman's effort to translate Vallejo's poetry, the hypocrisy of government officials and cultural bureaucrats, and finally, the paradox of Catholicism itself, its crushing injunctions against sexual freedom, its absorption of local myth and ritual into its own ceremonies.

One of his journal entries records the sacrifice of a sheep to honor his visit to a village. After bleeding, the animal's stomach was removed because a sac within "contains poisons & should it burst while in the stomach the meat

would be ruined." In dreaming of the slaughter several days
later, the image of the stomach reappears as a portion of
brain tissue, as if the removal of the stomach were, in the
dream's imagery, equivalent to passion or instinct which
religion cut out of awareness. "Without its stomach," he
noted, "the sheep's body seemed vacant—barren—almost
weightless." "I think Blake locates the stomach as 'hell,' "
and by such equations, Eshleman interprets the dream: the
sheep was the contemporary self, a figure eviscerated of its
instinctual nature, which might otherwise burst and "spoil"
thought. Eshleman then wrote in his journal,

> Why must I give up hell to live within love? Does
> Yorunomado [his imaginative comrade in *Indiana* and
> *Coils*] mean that my sense of love is narrow and thus
> will not include hell? Now if I think of hell as a place,
> symbolic as well as terrestrial, I can understand that—
> but Blake has so redefined hell as a positive force in
> creation that I have to take that meaning into con-
> sideration too. Must I kill my own energy—my
> furnaces—to be able to love?

Catholicism was like a membrane stretched around a core
of dark thought forcing civilization to deny half its wisdom
and experience. Vallejo's energy came from the vigor of his
penetration downward under the Catholic burden of guilt
and rejection to his Indian psyche, the buried, impacted
truth of Peruvian imagination. The tearing into a kind of
sac of powers within the self drove language into distorted,
animistic structures, grotesque and deformed tropes. The
poem was thus a kind of bursting of a sac of forbidden thinking, in which actuality suddenly ruptured and a grotesque
inner world leapt into language.

On Mules Sent from Chavin records Eshleman's attempt to "crawl out of the middlewestern bottleneck" of
his childhood rearing, while following Vallejo through layers
of Catholic colonial experience to a substratum of primitive

origins, the primal Incan world. In his introduction, Eshleman defines the world he had come from when he entered Peru:

> . . . I was brought up in the 40's in an anesthetically-clean Presbyterian home where smoking, drinking, swearing and gambling were not permitted, where I was an only child who was not allowed to play with Catholics, Jews, Negroes, children younger or older than I was, children whose parents smoked, drank, etc., or whose mothers wore slacks away from home. In a way, I was only permitted to be with those who were my "doubles"—children whose backgrounds, church and home lives were carbon copies of my own. A peculiar kind of Narcissism, in other words, based not upon looking into or at oneself but at others whose souls and potential human identities had been masked, mirroring my own masked identity.
>
> (12)

The making of a poet is dramatized in "The Book of Yorunomado" as the slashing, hara-kiri style, at the poet's own belly to release a force at the core of being, the ghost of Vallejo, whom he calls "Yorunomado" after the Japanese coffee house, "Nightwindow," where the drama is set. This is the "torn caul," a trope that appears frequently in the poetry of the early 1970s. The livingroom window at 4705 Boulevard Place, his parents' home in Indianapolis, was an early image of the membrane holding back thought from actuality; it overlooked the Butler Woods, and many of his lyric reminiscences call up the image of himself as a boy staring out from the interiors of his "anesthetically-clean Presbyterian" cell. Almost from the beginning his poetry turned on the central motif of a high wall whose perimeters he circled, looking for a door, windows, or opening; hell was the truth hidden, separated, negated by enclosures. The wall runs throughout his work, and figures prominently in his best book with its strategic title, *Fracture*.

Eshleman left Peru and proceeded to New York where he underwent Reichian therapy for two years, a process he likened to excavations through layers of trauma and sexual restraint to the self below. Eshleman had discovered the medical equivalent of Vallejo's inward journeys, as the therapy sessions became acts of psychological translation of an interior, trapped psyche. Like the Vallejo translations, these events and trials on Dr. Sidney Handleman's couch are striking emblems of postmodern activity: the naked Eshleman reduced to thumb-sucking and cooing, flexing his legs up and down and breathing under the parental gaze of his doctor—as he explored his childhood and distant beginnings. The transformation he experienced in these two years—a mixture of effects from Reichian treatments, new lovers, and his continuing efforts at translation—called to mind the pupa stages of a butterfly. When Eshleman began his own journal in 1967, he called it *Caterpillar,* and subtitled it, "A Gathering of the Tribes." The descent to one's interiors reversed the course of an aloof, abstract, racially defined ego; instead, one rediscovered the pooling of thought in the collective imagination. *Caterpillar* set out to prove Rothenberg's original thesis of the "deep image," that beneath the long cultural tradition of Western thought lay a wealth of discarded imagery depicting a unified species. "The gathering of the tribes" was possible only through psychological descents.

The arrival of *Caterpillar* on the New York scene in 1967 picked up postmodern writing in a period of flagging energies; many of the original reviews had already died, the literary energies of the movement ebbing as generational tribalism took a new form in the more popular arts of rock music, open theater, mass rallies, demonstrations, festivals, happenings, cult movies, and the like. The commercial exploitation of the movement had transformed the original renaissance into a media event for television, Hollywood treatments, fashion designers, magazine features. Major figures like Ginsberg, Kerouac, and Ken Kesey were now idols of the "youth culture," and what had originally been a post-war celebration of local and native traditions now became a highly channeled, outwardly-directed political movement against the war in Vietnam. Though the movement itself had not died, it had obliquely transformed itself from a celebration of national diversity into a protest against American imperialism in Asia. Power had shifted from England to America, and the artistic response changed accordingly—from open-ended experimentalism to celebrations of the arts and religions of subjugated cultures. Eshleman's international literary interests allowed him to take a leading role in reviving and refocusing postmodern writing from the late 1960s on.

Caterpillar sifted out a new mood in the second stage of the literary movement; much recessed behind the louder public phase of the Sixties, this other mood was dark and full of foreboding, a Cassandra voice of dire prophecies and painful, anguished self-analyses. Olson's earlier optimism had given way to misgivings:

> Call the Mouth the Place of Suffering
> Toothache's only a part of it.
>
>   I mean the bite,
> muscles that clamp down & shape the lips,
>
> show where the passionate endure their energies
> & the passive put up with what happens.

So wrote Robert Kelly in "Fire Famine," the opening poem in *Caterpillar* 14 (1971). Later in the same issue, Theodore Enslin's long sequence, "Synthesis, Part III," reads in part:

> To establish the link
> of an unbroken continuum
> becomes the guiding passion,
> or by its principle a man lives
> when all other ways of living
> have become impossible.
> Whatever it was he wanted,
> he wants in other ways—now—
> wants it out.
> To test the iconography of
> his going there—
> > to touch
> on many symbols, looking for the key
> which will unlock it—
> or
> > what is it that remains to be done?
> It was in dreams at the first of it,
> and it ends—
> > in dreams.

Throughout the issues, Eshleman as editor and as poet recorded a darkening vision and a diminished idealism among the avant-garde; the poetry expressed a sense of paralysis or blocked emotions approached with anguish. Creeley's fragmented lyrics in *Words* (1967) and *Pieces* (1969) identified a widespread malaise in literature working its way into *Caterpillar*.

Eshleman found voices that expressed the mood of the whole nation: their rambling or fragmented monologs tried breaking through an empty surface language, inert and disconnected from memory or the unconscious, efforts that were the reverse of the government's political circumlocutions over war policy and its motives for suppressing public outcries against the violence. Poets struggled with the opacities of speech to discover underlying psychological truths, which indirectly satirized government testimony in the Watergate hearings, where motives and specific facts regarding break-ins, domestic espionage, dirty tricks were neutralized in carefully composed statements in bureaucratese. On both sides of the fence, poets and government officials wrestled with the constraints of language, and both sides seemed mired in a slough of riddles and contradictions obscuring psychological truth.

Eshleman's *The Gull Wall* (1975), published two years after the close of *Caterpillar*, forms its theme out of a sense of inaccessibly remote psychological realities. The title piece, a prose meditation that ends in a long lyrical strophe, dwells on Paul Blackburn as a figure of the age, the segmented man whose instinctuality and self-knowledge were blunted into vicariousness, the suffering lover and voyeur of women he had abstractly deified and misconstrued. His notational verses add up to a self-portrait of a captive spirit scrutinizing the emotional life outside himself, a perceptive but uninvolved presence in the throng. Eshleman's lyric close imagines a sort of rescue for Blackburn, who has become a sea gull now, a Thoth-like spirit whom Eshleman escorts to the "Cavern of Self," where the contraries within him will thaw and presumably reconstruct him as a liberated soul: "he entered it, his back lost in the echoing struggle."

A year after *Caterpillar*'s close, Eshleman had come to the end of certain themes in his poetry. The autobiographical materials had been organized into a Romantic narrative of self-discovery, a transformation from conventional midwesterner to an artist in the currents of international thought. The theme was central to American Postmodernism, but in four major books and a dozen minor ones, the structure of the narrative had been fully fleshed. *The Gull Wall*, though brimming with possibilities, is thematically diffuse, a collection of poems mixing autobiography with portraits of a variety of artists whose collective energy is a pervasive, liberating force moving through the age. Van Gogh, Rimbaud, Artaud, Vallejo,

Charlie Parker, Bud Powell, Leon Golub, Francis Bacon, and
Blackburn all help to generate Eshleman's esthetic perspective. In "The Ronin Cock," the closing poem, he tells us, "I
was not merely a passage / through which life flowed, / I
began to feel I was attached / to some being which sent its
life / through me."

The poems of *The Gull Wall* cast about for a new way
to treat personal experience, to push conventional memory
beyond its narrow range of egocentric data toward an evolutionary memory. "I contain / a surreal grotesque," he wrote
in "Portrait of Francis Bacon," but

> can I make it stick
> against the wind—
> tunnel of our great
>
> abstract age?

> (*TGW* 98)

A shallow memory, like the impoverished modern consciousness, is cramped behind the accumulated denials of
a core of human mystery relating to animal origins; dreams
and intuitions are relics of that older memory, but such content is ignored in all other social activities except the arts.
The expanded consciousness occurs only through liberation
of the deeper memory; even though its content is encoded
in riddling archetypes, they are the principal keys for in-
terpreting one's psychic experience. Without them one is
set adrift in life where only the ego's reality is confirmed.
The archetypal memory grasps the cyclical events of nature,
in which life suddenly becomes strange and magical again:

> I know that bone
> cave where Ulysses
> lies face down in body

sludge, his arm
around his drunken
comrade Elpenor,
I have felt them crawled

by diamond-backed
maggots, and I have heard
the hags laugh
who crouch

about them, senile
and pregnant,
the *grotesca* who link
Rabelais Goya and Artaud

(TGW 98-99)

The deep memory of the past is compacted into the term "hell" in Christian dogma, and a great range of archetypal experience is thus stored in what we call the realm of damnation. Accordingly, to sin is to regress psychologically into earlier modes of identity, in which the isolated consciousness begins merging again with the natural forms it had renounced. Hell is thus the core of nature, the life force at the stem of memory, where identity breaks down into the animal continuum. Virtue and grace are Christian ideals of abstract and remote human perfection, the soul rising out of the stews of nature into a realm of idea, reflection, disembodied intellection. Eshleman set out to explore the psychological interiors of damnation in order to prove that hell was in fact the dark corridors of human evolution, whose spiraling passages up through nature had already been "mapped" by the grotesque tradition.

The seeds of Eshleman's new strategy lay in various Romantic texts, in particular Blake's "Marriage of Heaven and Hell." But Goethe's *Faust* was also part of the moral background of his scheme: Faust was the flower of

European Enlightenment thought, the pride of Germany, but an empty, isolated man devoid of sensuality. Goethe's play is an indictment of the half-man created by 18th century rationalism. The devil alone could restore the nature missing in this blighted ideal who would, by century's end, become the hapless and corrupted figure of Conrad's Mr. Kurtz. Faust bartered his intellectual life, his "soul," for the sake of a sexual encounter, and later, for marriage to Helen of Troy, the pagan feminine ideal. Eshleman's own thesis goes even farther, that hell itself is the abyss in which consciousness can heal itself, regain its lost impulses, desires, instinctuality, and thus reenter life.

Eshleman wanted his poetry to expose Christianity as a religion of fear and loathing, a theology that concealed its dread of nature in an elaborate allegory that depicted heaven as the highest reaches of intellect and hell as the lowest depths of instinctual degradation. That vastly distorted duality was at the heart of contemporary sterility, and only by turning the meaning of hell inside out could one reclaim the mystery of nature that was sacred to most other religions, those that Western imperialism had set out to destroy and replace with Christian dogma. The fiercely negative valuation of "hell" functioned as a sort of "plug" against the past, preventing any form of regression from making its appeals to a thinly fabricated sense of self as a thing apart. Western civilization had defined itself through a process of disengagements from the environment, with hell as the center of degraded nature. Hence, the destruction of the eco-system and the aggressions against primitive cultures of the Third World had as their primary motivation the strengthening of identity through annihilation of natural and human otherness. By pulling the "plug," and thus reversing the valuation of hell, one could oppose the fatal momentum of Western thought and expose its threat of nuclear holocaust as a form of racial paranoia threatening the world.

It remained for Eshleman to ground these and other speculative readings on the formation and biases of Western thought. Eshleman needed the evidence of specific cultural contexts in which the psychological function of hell could be shown at work. In 1974, he came across the Russian critic Mikhail Bakhtin's study, *Rabelais and His World,* which discovers a relationship between the grotesque humor and exaggeration of Rabelais' satire and the erotic licence of medieval carnival fête, the seasonal and feast-day rituals of European village life. In such rites, the celebrants wore masks and affected disfiguring appearances or disguised themselves in animal costumes and fell into a state of lawless abandon, which even civil authorities tolerated. Bakhtin argues that such behavior was a throwing off of the burdens of civil life, of social hierarchy, and religious restraint. Rabelais marks the end of the era of such carnival purgations, but Eshleman saw at once an instance of ritual surrender to the abyss, a plunging of villagers into primordial freedom. Their costumes and sexual humors were a revel in lower states of mind, to vent the pressures of city life. Rabelais' own satiric humors were assaults upon the musty, narrow theology of Catholicism in the High Renaissance, of which the Abaye de Thélème is a corrective ideal. But already a paler, more subdued form of satire was replacing Rabelais' barbarous hyperbole and low comedy, in which the excretory functions of the "lower body" formed a central motif. Bakhtin's study gave Eshleman a necessary perception into hell's therapeutic powers for a society staggering under its moral and ethical restraints.

The imagery of entangled life forms, the "grotesque archetype," was present among such *carnivalistes,* as human beings sprouted antlers, horns, tails, fur, elongated limbs, a spectacle of human deformities which bore all the evolutionary chaos of Christian fears of hell. The carnival mood, according to Bakhtin, was an episode in the "history of laughter," in which the primordial spirit in human life found its voice and ridiculed the pressures of civilization. One of the latent assumptions of Bakhtin's study is that a side of consciousness resents and insults the forces willfully molding human nature outside the flux of other life. Laughter had its own archetypal springs, its link to pre-conscious existence. But the question remained, what was the basis of such archetypes? Was hell possibly a mental projection of lost experience, an actual event codified in archetypal form?

In 1974, Eshleman made his first trip to the caves of the Dordogne region in southwestern France, where Upper Paleolithic human cultures had resided among the honeycomb passages of the limestone outcroppings. Many of the caves followed the course of the Vézère River and formed the perimeters of a cultural enclave distinguished for its prolific wall painting and bas-relief designs. The most elaborate works were found in the "Hall of Bulls" at Lascaux, known as the "Sistine Chapel" of cave art, discovered in 1940. It ranks with the paintings discovered at Altamira a half-century before; but Lascaux seemed reserved for postmodernist treatment, and Eshleman quickly perceived that here, in primordial figures and scrawls, were acts of mind in which the underworld was first taking form.

By striking coincidence, the caves very nearly formed the basements and undercrofts of the Catholic churches above them. The bold, bright figures of animals, rendered in manganese, vegetable dyes, and possibly urine and blood, possessed the crude, emphatic profiles found in stained-glass windows. The use of the caves as initiation centers made them the first cathedrals of Europe, an anticipation by thirty-five thousand years or more of the cultural patterns of the Christian era. As Eshleman became familiar with the paintings, he realized he had discovered a lode of archetypal figures at their inception. The entangled life forms and the tentative emergence of a first human portrait in the "dancing sorcerer" established this art as the human nursery of thought, the record kept of the dawning of consciousness. Eshleman disputed the scholarly interpretations of cave art as reflections on hunting life; in his prefaces to *Hades in Manganese* (1981) and *Fracture* (1983), he argues persuasively that cave art formed the human diary of primordial awareness. The dark caverns, the "litho-uterine" coils and canals which primal humanity squeezed through to construct its murals, imprinted themselves on human memory as the landscape of hell. The trip to the Dordogne had proven that hell was not merely a conceptual framework vaguely hinting of origins; hell was the dwelling place of human life at about 35,000 B.C., in which the actual events, surprise encounters with bears, clashes with other tribes, fires and smokey caverns, flickering light and the echoing of voices, settled into mythic and archetypal recollections that later civilizations distilled as the dread fate of backsliders to social evolution. The dungeon is a form of that dread, an earthly punishment to the miscreants who had surrendered to retrograde desires. But even the cathedral is a form of the cave, in its echoing chambers, weak lights, vaulted ceilings and incense-laden rituals. The caves were central to the making of the European, i.e., Western psyche, and both its spiritual aspirations and worst fears were fitted into thought by the long sojourn in the limestone underworld of Paleolithic culture.

Under the cathedral pediments of Catholic France, Spain, and Italy ranged the beginnings of human awareness and the actual mazes of hell. In 1978 Eshleman came upon another crucial text for his thesis, James Hillman's *The Dream and the Underworld,* in which literary references to the underworld are closely compared to processes and structures of mind, thus arguing a connection between sets of metaphoric description pointing back to lived experience. Hillman's thesis suggested that the conception of mind itself was modelled upon a particular set of circumstances—the events by which a groping, inchoate sensibility was seized by a new and disorienting power—the ability to transfer immediate sensation into likenesses, a passing of the quick of nature into the inertness of rock walls. For Eshleman, the moment posed as many threats as it promised triumphs of human will. The capacity to represent the natural world pried apart the continuum that held humanity in paradisal relation. The separation between a thinking power and the muteness of nature could only result in enmity and spiritual warfare thereafter. The caves birthed a spirit of revenge which wreaked its havoc the more the chasm widened between nature and the human being. The function of religion was to keep open the breach in life, to seal the wound on either side and goad the spirit upward out of the organic world. The function of grotesque art was to preserve what connections it could between the old continuum and the withering sensibilities of modern life.

The artists and writers Eshleman found useful represent the force of reconciliation with the natural world; these are the heretics whose works argued for a transvaluation of cultural history; the past was not the negative gradients marking the progress of mankind, but a winding maze of confused attempts to escape from reality, the web of living things. By the mid-1970s, Eshleman's interest had shifted to the example of Antonin Artaud, a martyr to the cause, whose years of incarceration and shock-therapy were efforts to silence France's boldest adversary of modern culture. Artaud was at the front lines of the oldest battle of history: resisting the final assault of rationalism against what remained of human nature. Artaud's "mature poetry (1945–48)," Eshleman wrote in the introduction to his translations of *Antonin Artaud: 4 Texts* (1982), "is a multifoliate binding of attraction/repulsion for virtually all the materials and sensations that the poet is conscious of. The friction created by Artaud's unceasing induction and cursing of the physical world is in the service of opening up an underworld out of which a 'dark parturition of principles' can be summoned." Artaud's persona, the Mômo, functions as a kind of primal psyche, the activated memory of ancient life:

> If the enemy is the anchored mind (and by extension, in this poem, the sexually degraded body and ego), the victor, to the extent that there is one, is the Mômo itself, . . . a monstrous presence, but its monstrosity is not simply that of deformity and pain . . . but a delirious inherence as well as a sophisticated critic of all reductions of the whirling dervish of the soul.

Though poetry specifically dealing with the caves abounds by 1977, in *Grotesca* and *Core Meander* and in the major collection of 1978, *What She Means*, a unified argument of their significance to the modern self is first formulated in *Hades in Manganese*, which narrates a modern descent into the Dordogne underworld. In the opening poem, "Lich Gate," Eshleman buries his former self in the churchyard, "the outer hominid limit." This burial is a kind of reversal: in putting his former life into the ground, it will sprout its true vitalities in the other realm. The modern self is the dead one, a figure born of stifled natural affinities; ego or person are ghostly fictions, and in burying them, one replanted a seed. In "Hades in Manganese," the long, anchoring poem of the text, "self" is identified as the "apex of pain." "Why," he asks, "do we treat the hero / better than he treated the material / he severed to feed the sun?" Eshleman's visionary quest is:

> . . . not another bringing of the dark
> up into the light, but a dark
> delivered dark paleolithic imagination.

(H 41)

"If there must be clarity," he notes in "Winding Windows," "Let it be opaque, let the word be / as translucent as night starred" (69).

Poetry is redefined as "racemose," that is, as roots of thought going into nature, not as discriminations brought to finer and finer focus of thought:

> Take this intercourse and let it wind
> back to previous being,
> suffering landed dryness,
>
> eating its way back to
> brine in the body of another.
> To be born is to bear being enclosed,
>
> to eat into a hearing, less a being
> heard than ear tripping seeing,
> so that sight falls here and finds
>
> its limit. The image of an outline
> vibrates back to its first
> disappearance, fanged hand notched
>
> bone.

(H 75)

In "The Aurignacians Have the Floor," dedicated to Gary Snyder, Eshleman begins, "Now I subtract myself from the industrial / white hive," the endproduct of Western civilization, and concludes by declaring:

> I will accept the Aurignacian motion
> that the abyss is engravable
> and terminates in caves manifesting
>
> hominid separation.
>
> (*H* 91)

The abyss leads to a reorganization of values, a decon-
structed selfhood that partly meets up with its opposities,
and in which the awareness of the historic dimension is keen-
ly heightened for the poet:

> Each word, then, is a shaft,
> a jumbled midden, in which most of the bones
> are red deer.
>
> Read dear.
>
> (*H* 113)

Two years later, in *Fracture,* the image of the abyss as a
recombinant chamber of the soul grows even bolder:

> In the vortex of the whirlpool below,
> animals are separating and recombining with men—
> the archetypal grotesque is constant
> from Lascaux to Disneyland, intersected by Rabelais,
> by Belsen, by gargoyles
> poised for eternity on the periphery of the holy,
> that periphery is the furrow in which
> the crossbreeding of the marvelous takes place
>
> (*F* 143)

In *Fracture*'s central poem, "Visions of the Fathers
of Lascaux," Eshleman puts together his entire perspective
to describe the birth of the human soul in the stone womb
of Lascaux. The poem is a *tour de force* of lyrical synthesis;
the Christian version of genesis is the foil to his cave thesis

as Eshleman constructs a commentary on the fate of the soul wrenched from the "caul" of nature. This forced birth out of darkness and natural innocence was an act of unknowing will, a rude awakening of dream-entangled beings, in which the sequence of evolutionary steps leading up to contemporary life produced only a deformed, fragmentary being. The half-soul that emerged turns against the natural world around it, bent upon its destruction. Eshleman views the whole of human history as a Gothic tale of some ghoulish being wreaking its havoc upon unconscious life. His narrative develops a cartoon-like satiric fantasy on human evolution, as here, in his treatment of the origins of human hierarchical society:

> At the base of this pyramid
> the King of Cracked Morning slept
> lifting his loaded sleeve occasionally
> to direct the ant-like orchestration of slaves
> mounting peak after peak thinking
> as they struggle across solar plains they are building
>   cities.
> Evil increases relative to the steepness of the pyramid,
> its latest peak is now at our throats
> as we gaze down the steps of any ruin
> it is only Kashkaniraqmi who casts an archeological
>   veil across the steps
> to hide the bloody chewed out teeth
> the stains of dark blue amputated limbs
> mossed with gangrene that cover each ascent

(F 68)

The deepest past is not a pastoral Eden, a romantic illusion of "some farfetched purity or chaos," but

the heaving nucleus of femur set in bear eye socket
          burials
words inserted through the openings of a resistance
strong enough to hold his poem in place
even though the prisoner within the prisoner is the
          colonial target of ring
upon narrowing ring to
the strong central suck of a pupil
frosted, still alive
which I float into,
more into cooked marrow than in the language rubble
          of a bison staring

(F 69)

The close of this extraordinary poem involves a final subplot, the installation in the mind of "Lascaux," the Adamic exile, of a dream residue of life before the "fall." The three magi who created him break Lascaux's beak, "using it as an engraving tool / to slash their roan colorings in the tunnel seams, / with manganese and ochre dioxide / they drilled language deposits into these seams" lest all trace of their act be forgotten. So the poem is that memory revivified, gleaned from the walls of Lascaux.

One may find here all of Eshleman's influences brought to bear upon his central text: the allegorical narrative mode of Blake, the twisted, distorted image clusters of Vallejo, the dream patterning Hillman explored, the two-way currents of memory between the abyss and modern consciousness traced by Bakhtin, Olson's use of myth to pattern and interpret modern experience, and Eshleman's own elaborate sexual perspective on the nature of modern alienation, together with Reich, and even Blackburn, who appears heavily disguised here as Lascaux, the beaked human. The poem attempts a narrative of human genesis in which the Romantic tradition is merged with the long view of the biological revolution; it uses the arguments and positions of many disciplines that have sprung up since Darwin set in motion his thesis on human origin.

But its foremost purpose is to dramatize the events that gave the Western spirit its destructive and isolating tendencies leading to the Atomic Age. The main thrust of postmodernism was to celebrate native cultures suppressed by Western imperial tradition; but Eshleman went beyond his colleagues in fixing the date of human genesis further back in history, and by tracing the root of Western alienation to a primordial rupture in the natural continuum. The consequence, as he saw it, was a narcissistic culture that soon came to loathe the reality that contradicted its aloof imagination. The flower of human artificiality was the white Anglo-Saxon idealization of self, the product of the ethnocentric world of British imperialism and the long tradition of Western philosophy that defined the ego as the pinnacle of Western identity. Hell was the spiral stairs which humanity had climbed to arrive at catastrophic alienation; Eshleman's siftings of esthetic dissent brought him to the conclusion that the way up could be reversed.

The poetry ending this century is very different from the English symbolism closing the last with its distillations and "silverpoints" of verse. So eclectic is the present mode, in fact, that the critic Mary Kinzie was provoked to attack John Ashbery for his "obsessive promiscuity of styles," to which Eshleman responded that such "fear [which] the self-righteous have at the sight of the high mixing with the low" has "led the world to its present peril" (Kinzie, "The Rhapsodic Fallacy," *Salmagundi* [Feb., 1984]). But in the best hands, there seems to be infinite variety of execution, a dazzling flexibility to map and record the subtlest nuance and shift of thought, the most delicate labyrinth of sensation and idea, the feeblest signal from the brain to the language center. It is all picked up, the mind having become transparent in this late, mature poetry of the century of self-analysis. Such poetry, wrote Eshleman recently, "attempts to be responsible for all an individual writer knows about himself and about his world. It is that awesome. It is a poetry of wrath rather than instruction, ambivalent about all the major movements of right before its own time, and it reveals depths and abysses of human nature that only the isolated Blake and elderly Goya, to name two great 18th century outsiders, depicted." Such poetry intended to plumb recesses and remote zones of human sensibility mostly ignored or censored. Again, Eshleman is pointed and explicit: "Such a state of awareness [required in the new poetry] would in varying degrees be contingent upon the writer's feeling for and understanding of his own physical body, especially in our limboless Protestant society, his physical lower body, still the most inaccessible stronghold of material that has been stigmatized as unacceptable to literature" ("Response to Mary Kinzie," *Sulfur 13*). Styles range from the trance-like marginal voice of daydreams in Ashbery, to the splintered quick-change thinking in August Kleinzhaler's *Earthquake Weather*. At the mainstream is Eshleman's own mingling of tones and sonorities, whose torrents of speech mix dream logic with crisply worded argument or shatter narrative with oblique flashes of memory and grotesque fantasy.

The first wave of postmodernists drew on the ideogrammic style of Pound, Williams, and the Objectivists; their short, staggered strophes emphasized the sufficiency of objective description in establishing a system of relations among objects. Those verbal "nodes" represented the objects themselves; a page was thus a landscape on which verbal equivalents of objects were placed. The reader entering such a page of landscape is required to infer from the location and latent interactiveness of the "objects" what their cumulative relations signify. The ideogram reversed the expository means of traditional lyric discourse; the verbalized objects are sufficient declarers of meaning in themselves, and if one could develop meaning merely by juxtaposing two or more objects in an environment, the result proved a multitude of propositions crucial to postmodern ideology. Nature formed itself, and as Olson had suggested in "Projective Verse," the role of the "objectist" artist is to reenact events from natural landscapes, so as to overhear "the secrets objects share." The ideogram implied that the objects of nature were animate, and that spirit inhered in matter as much as in sentient living beings. The ideogram made the same propositions Whitehead argued in *Process and Reality,* in that all objects possessed a will toward coherent structures and entered into them by a natural dynamism. Poetry of the first wave of writers thus figured as landscapes in which the clustered language formed the objects of extended ideograms; their juxtapositions set up paths of semantic interaction that worked up as well as down the page, the way an actual landscape would accumulate a range of dynamic connections for a person observing it from various angles. The ideogrammic projections of poetry closed a gap between Western discourse and the animism of primitive cultures; both attested to the autonomy of nature where humans were eavesdroppers and respectful onlookers. Meaning arose from the internal discourse of objects communicating their spiritual affinities which human perception partly deciphered. Hence, the principle of discontinuity in ideogrammic lyricism, which not only pictured the objects themselves but the discontinuous mode of a human being perceiving their relations taking form.

But a new wave of postmodern writers surrounding Eshleman perceived a dichotomy within consciousness itself—between the orderly psyche shaped by Western social ideals and an underlying nature largely cut-off from articulation. It was this core of instinct and intuition that became in their poetry a second self whose roots were in nature and in others. Their poetry dropped the structures of ideogrammic writing to engage in a dialogical discourse in which the inner, second self burst through the partitions of rational discourse and often flooded reason and orderly argument with its erotic or animistic tirades, its disclosures of a hidden life in nature in which others were part of its essential identity. Eshleman's poem "Manticore Vortex," in *Fracture*, summarizes at least part of the dichotomous relations of the new poetry:

> The self is an active cannibalism of its own matrix
> and the co-producer of its birth
> To the visitor it would appear as if there were only
> a large bolted screw in this basement floor,
> but there is Aztec density here.
> A pubescent boil has been transformed into a crystal
>   ball
> through which the poem sees the guardian rattler
> dreaming at the Amerindian stratum of the world
>
>   (*F* 143)

The second wave of poetry moves in long discursive strophes and involves a format of initial inducements to coax out the inner, second self, whose monolog is the essential goal of the poem. This interior voice of frustrated nature resembles what in primitive society would be a whole and healthy identity, but which comes to us in the poetry as an encysted ghostly otherness torn by repression and rational tyranny, but who takes the stage once coaxed up out of the lower stratum of the poet's psyche. In that way, the new poetry moves back toward symbolist discourse, and sets up a series of correspondences between ruling and subject selves, as though the interior self were a captive or slave of the governing role of the ego. The relations between ego and human nature mimic those of Western powers and colonialists, but the poems dramatize the superior strength and character of the second self, whose emergence in the trance-states of the poem constitutes a near overthrow of rationality, or at least an invasion and temporary disruption of power. Many times the poems close in a draw between selves or a surrender of human nature to its guardian ego. In any case, the second wave of postmodernism refigured the terms of a relation set up by the first—and both generations of poets agreed in essence on the fundamental dichotomy of Western awareness and the autonomy of nature. The first group put nature outside and in the form of self-creating wholes of an actual landscape; the other group found nature within, under the rule of rational intellect. Eshleman's generation gave the second self many names, depending on the psychological tenets of one's poetry: it was the feminine side, the remnants of paleolithic holism, the dark other, the wild but entrapped nature bound in Reichian armor, the lost id, the squandered energies of the collective unconscious. But it was there, and served to represent all of nature beyond self: it was the animate, spiritually rich object of nature within, which borrowed the intellect's own tongue to voice itself in those lyrical expostulations swelling from the strophes of their poems.

In his "Response to Mary Kinzie," Eshleman complains that critics like Kinzie, Helen Vendler, and Harold Bloom continue to separate and make hierarchies of content, whereas the new "configuration of poetics" over the last fifty years or so has in fact resolved extremes and made a bond of emotional and intellectual content. To learn this new art of synthesis the young writer should study the "texts of Bakhtin, Ferenczi and [James] Hillman" instead of going off to the "creative writing wards." This is a "Dionysian poetry," not an Apollonian mode of certainty, absolutes, explanations. "20th century poetry is a rain forest as well as a new wilderness," and the critic who asks to read it must be "willing to take on material that makes [one] stretch to [one's] last zoa, but also to accept archetypal psychology, insanity, archeology, slavery, anti-semitism and Capitalism as standard and active equipment of literary response."

The synthesizing tendencies of Eshleman's poetic even draw on a new form of the poem, "the middle-length poem (not a lyric but not an epic)," in the manner of rhapsody, the word Olson unravelled to reclaim its original Greek meaning as "songs stitched together," and which Eshleman now calls "our presiding archetypal pattern!" Bringing us toward the rhapsodic pattern, the "middle-length poem," is a converging heritage of international poetics which Eshleman traced to "César Vallejo, Aimé Césaire, Charles Olson, Antonin Artaud, Octavio Paz, Robert Duncan, Paul Celan, and Vladimir Holan." But the list extends to many more poets, including Paul Blackburn, Corman, Snyder, Creeley, Kelly, Michel Deguy, and others. This poetry, he writes, constitutes "the shattered lantern glass of previous hermetics," and "is much more concerned with process than with product," an Olsonian premise. Eshleman goes on to say that all of this heritage may be called "Abstract Romanticism," a hybrid denomination intended to suggest a parallel with abstract expressionism, and which combines visionary elements of traditional romantic poetry with the discontinuities and oblique arguments of contemporary discourse.

Poetry has always possessed healing power, a function emphasized throughout the Romantic tradition. The evolution of recent poetics has turned the techniques and linguistic structure of the poem exclusively to this purpose; no portion of the poem remains outside the act of self-recovery. The entire content of the poem bends to its desired goal, and as such, the contemporary poem may have arrived at a point at which it resembles the exorcism rites of ancient cultures. Put another way, the poem has so combined its elements as to approximate religious ritual, and to have the same purport: the redemption of the soul. The contemporary poem reverses the Christian act of absolution; its form of redemption is to arouse the flesh and merge it with the soul, thus aligning it with much older religions and the primordial mind. "I write free-ing / to free the Beast Spirit," Michael McClure noted in his "Statement on Poetics" in Allen's anthology. A decade later, Eshleman wrote at the end of *Altars,* "My poetics are the oldest and most engaging human adventure: the emancipation of the self."

Chapter Two

A Poetics of the Body

me too, a caterpillar, and as I
passed through myself
a pair of blood spats remained.

"Variations Done for John Digby" (*WSM* 155)

The "G.I. Bill," passed in 1944, performed a bloodless surgery on America's institutions of higher learning. Colleges that could not change curricula quietly perished; those that could, threw out the liberal arts courses in Latin, Greek, Geography, Ancient History, Music, and wrote up new training programs in bureaucratic organization and management. College now became the temple of the middle class; the gentry supported a few private institutions for its own, but even these would bend and grow in the direction of the federally-mandated curriculum. High school lost its function as the instrument which trained the semi-skilled for factory work: the bells and lock-step discipline drove a dispirited class now demoted to a lower social rung. Dropping out, vandalism, early marriage were some of the consequences of working-class alientation in the Cold War years. Half of high school became the preparatory track for college study: its courses anticipated the new college curriculum ahead, while youths of both classes, laboring and managerial, thronged the same crowded halls. The so-called rebel of the Fifties was a manifestation of labor class resentment against the rise of the new technicians: the shaggy-haired, leather-jacketed "hood" stood up for proletarian values when he jeered at and rejected the pretensions of a new technological elite in America. The virtues of strength and bravery, manual dexterity and cunning were replaced by a sudden reverence for mental skills and organizational loyalties. The high school became the fault line of the two classes, the one in decline after centuries of respect, the other eager to spend money on the sudden plenty of post-WWII prosperity, to consume the luxuries and gadgets flooding into the market. It was a generation that did not look back, but forward to a peacetime that promised leisure, security, and a continuation of Anglo-American bonds.

No one could say specifically what was missing in life, only that it was altered and the young had to find their way in it. The culture of America was no longer differentiated into small towns and backwater villages; the war had pulled young men and women out of the side-streets into the mainstream economy. The nation's diverse communities had become unified by radio and newspaper networks. The life of isolated communities was drawn into a national life, and those who returned from war had seen the world, and had come home restless, critical, uneasy. The novelties of post-war life were welcomed into the household, but the old morality still applied, and children chafed against the inconsistencies of their rearing. These and other forces converged to weaken family ties—a situation endlessly repeated in the melodramas of film, radio, televison, pulp fiction, and magazine articles.

Novels began appearing which featured a prototype of the young rebel. First came the young anti-hero Holden Caulfield of *Catcher in the Rye* (1951) by J. D. Salinger; Kerouac carefully documented the disintegration of the family in his autobiographical novel, *The Town & The City* (1950), in which a stifling conventionality and sterility represent home and town (Lowell, Massachusetts), while reckless freedom marked the city to which his young protagonist ultimately flees. The decision to escape is difficult, but celebrated once set in motion. John Clellon Holmes's *Go* (1952) is a powerful evocation of the city in the 1950s—a landscape of social fluidity, anonymity, sexual adventure, where old values had broken down and the young explored the limits of their independence. The city was rootless, a maze where an itinerant generation milled about, always transient, always unpredictable. Kerouac's *On the Road* (1957) depicts the major cities of the U.S. as ports of call for his nomadic cast as they roam coast to coast looking for "kicks" and "thrills." The same characters emerge from each of these picaresque novels—prodigals from small towns and middle class home-life, angry at a culture that misunderstood them, anxious to become artists. By the mid-1950s, a popular version of the hero was full fledged and recognizable in various media—a white, middle-class youth in his teens or early twenties, brooding, inarticulate, erotically charismatic. This ideal was embraced across the nation as youngsters flocked to the movies to watch their hero take form in Marlon Brando and James Dean, to read about him in new novels by the Beats, or scrutinize his outbursts in the poems of Ginsberg, Ferlinghetti, and Corso. But the hero's outlook was more difficult to discern—it stood for an undefined independence—an adulthood beyond parental control and prior to marriage or material possessions, a murky interim without rules. Neal Cassady was the original of all these versions of the new rebel—his rootlessness and vitality were the marks of the time. He had no hometown and his loyalties were confined to the friends he made on the road; his element was a car hurtling down a freeway as he drank, talked, looked for adventure. Spontaneity, speed of thought, chatter, recklessness were elements of Cassady's aura—which Beat writers incorporated into fictional and poetic personae.

An intellectual fringe spanning various groups and movements across the country began speaking of a new mode of awareness, the phenomenological perception of objects and events Olson characterized as the "human universe." The duality of subject and object dissolves into phenomenological reality when surroundings and their multitudes of objects begin contributing to one's sense of self. The reanimation of an object demotes the centrality of self (and ego) essential to empirical reason. Objects cease to be mere counters and commodities as they become the active contents of one's sensibility. The identification of self or "I" with a natural object dissolves the very alienation on which technological exploitation depends. The self expands in consciouness through absorption of its environment, a linguistic transaction in which things are invested with the power of self and become the reciprocal forces in one's perceptions and identity. The act of re-animating inert phenomena broke open the Western sentence as a model of power relations between subject and object, redistributing the parts in a more dynamic relation. Linearity and progression were the linguistic conventions of an imperializing orthodoxy which phenomenological thought up-ended and reversed. The poem's structure now tended toward strophes of clustered imagery and data devoid of lyrical embellishment or re-arrangement of their actuality—Olson's *typos*, *topos*, and *tropos* of pure existence. The new poem reenacted an environment in the lay of its strophes and thickets of words—on which a poet's attention dwelt in forming its perceptions. The poem (and prose narrative) demonstrated the reciprocal nature of awareness between self and surroundings.

Throughout the decade closing scenes in both fiction and poetry depicted a mind in the embrace of its surroundings, the self "naturalized," transported out of "thought" into immediate, direct perception of phenomena. The orthodoxy Olson rejects in "Projective Verse" is not so much the closed conventions of Anglo-American poetry, but its implicit conclusion that the mind triumphs over nature through epiphanies and deductions, having solved the riddles of emotion and experience. The orthodox poem depicted a self in the shadowy natural world setting things right like a Sherlock Holmes, after which it could retreat to its intellectual citadel, secure in its logic and empirical certainty. The orthodox poem was another code for imperialism, a raid on experience in which the natural world was conquered and reduced to abstractions.

The popular appeal of Ginsberg and Kerouac went far to create a favorable image of the artist among the young. Art no longer seemed a medium of rarified ideas and visions but a vehicle for talking back to elders and to authority, a forum in which to "howl" at one's oppressors and mock the nation's humorless restraints and conventions. For the first time in American life, art liberated a wide range of middle class youths. And the integrated communications media of post-war America encouraged the rapid expansion of the youth movement; by the late 1950s, its allurements had seeped down into the heartland as far as Bloomington, Indiana, where Clayton Eshleman languished after earning his B.A. in philosophy in 1958. He had been chafing at his father's authoritarianism for years; the early poetry describes the strict constraints of home life firmly enforced by his parents' dread of new experience.

Whenever he stumbled into sexual knowledge, the voice of his father sounded nearby, turning the boy back. His anguished recollections of youth in later poetry show him padding up and down behind the window looking out to the Butler Woods, a park adjoining Butler University, where the green world stretched out toward freedom. Something else nagged more insistently at the young man which the poems also voice: the claustrophobia of being born inland, far from the sources of culture—at the tame heart of a continent in which life went on routinely in a community of shopkeepers and clerks, whose trim and orderly neighborhoods held back each new generation until it mellowed into genteel conformity. What really bored into the thoughts of a young writer at Bloomington—a name rich in possibilities for his artistic awakening—was that both coasts had produced a new art of striking possibilities among the young.

Although the "movement" as such was still in its infancy, the lines of its development were already clear and accessible through various magazines, most of which had been started in the 1950s. Eshleman would discover many of the leading figures of postmodernism in *Origin* (begun in Boston in 1951), *Big Table, Paris Review, Black Mountain Review* (begun at Black Mountain College in 1954 under Creeley's editorship), and *Evergreen Review,* jointly edited by Barney Rosset and Donald Allen, and started in 1957. Kelly, whom Eshleman was soon to meet, co-founded the *Chelsea Review* in New York in 1958, and edited *Trobar* in 1960. *Measure* was edited by John Weiners and began publication in Boston in 1957. On the West Coast, various magazines flourished briefly; among the more substantial were *The Ark* and *City Lights,* both in San Francisco.

The product of Eshleman's first labors is *Mexico & North,* printed in Kyoto, Japan, in 1962 at his own expense. Originally, it was to have been published by Kelly, who liked

the early poems and had encouraged Eshleman to complete
a book. But Kelly's interest waned, as Eshleman complains
in his poem "Divine Aid," included in *Coils*.

> Was Kelly a
> spiritual friend? Did he know something about
> *Mexico & North* I who wrote it did
> not? Why shd Kelly take the book
>
> & never write again? Or not for six months?
> Why shd Kelly my comrade hold
> my book, its miserable 200 copies, in.
>
> . . . Why shd Kelly hold my book? Was I a threat to
> Kelly? He had offered to *distribute* it. But before,
> a two years before, he had offered to
>
> publish it, then imprint it, then neither.

(*C* 36)

Mexico & North is apprentice work by a poet who read
carefully and absorbed the examples of his masters, Blake,
Whitman, Pound and Neruda, without quite feeling the
urgency of their ideas. His own situation is more compelling: a naive midwesterner afoot suddenly in the primal landscapes of Mexico and Taiwan, with his notebook ready and
his attention fixed on things he has never seen or imagined.
His regional life had not prepared him for a glimpse into
cultures that still lived in close alliance with the dark side
of the human psyche, with myth, ritual, violence, the suf-
ferings of poverty, neglect. This was elemental life—and he
took down his impressions in a manner close to Corman's
gists and carefully crafted phrases. The poems grow by the
phrase, not by the strophe or narrative frame. Here and
there the young Eshleman catches sight of paradox—a
drunken ceremony, animals milling in the household, squalid

houses and dirty children, life outside the boundaries of his own narrowly defined childhood.

The poems, all of them short and tightly worded, want to overcome an initial revulsion and perceive this "filthy matter" as medicine, the healing herbs of experience. Technically, the poems experiment with open form, but only casually. There is no deliberate effort to approximate Olson's projective mode of sprawling lines and strophes. Eshleman is comfortable spreading out the poem's form to emphasize the phrasing itself, to draw attention to the short staccato pace of language as it imitates the process of attention: the jerky shocks he felt looking into the lives of an alien landscape. Here is a kind of Candide loose in the orders of a collective social scheme, dumbfounded not at sin but at contradiction, the shocks to his own social gospel. The little book, though mildly argued and cautious in its surmises, offers a first portrait of a figure grappling with his emotional ignorance in a transparent lyric language.

Eshleman's persona is a far cry from the characters of Beat literature, who rushed into similar experience with great zest. Eshleman's character is more concerned to realize there is a knowledge that has been withheld from him, that a world existed beyond the boundaries of his own tightly-constricted monoculture. And already we may discern something of the motives of deep image writing—that sense of secretive life which the poet must hack at the undergrowth to encounter. Even in his nascent lyricism we find the deep image tucked away among the shacks, in the dark alleys and mysterious privacy of native life. This hidden world is the habitat of his own psyche—the terms of its own concealed existence within.

> white tissue hung
> from twine-web
> taut between houses . . .

grease!
urine, stacks
of pineapple chunks black
with bees

("Water Song," MN)

To stalk down the squalid details of a shanty town in Mexico is akin to Wakoski's persistent reconstruction of her father, the Navy officer away at sea most of her childhood, or of Rothenberg sorting the memories he has heard of Poland from parents and relatives. The secret of the true self lay in other landscapes, hidden among alien experience to which one has no easy access. Memory, dreams, waking fantasy are the only bridge between a shallow conscious self and the great expanse of the true psyche, between materialism and the depths of spirit in the soul. The search for the deep self that goes on in this early poetry of Eshleman and the others is goaded largely by despair. Hillman describes the mood of *Mexico & North* when he writes in *The Dream and the Underworld* that

> There is a curious correlation between feelings of reality about the underworld and feelings of value about the soul. It is as if, when we have no vivid imagination of the underworld, a flattening takes place, even a depersonalization that must be made good by Epicurean community and friendship—or what today is called "relating." The less underworld, the less depth, and the more horizontally spread out becomes one's life. The materialistic view ends in a kind of void, the very Halls of Hades now only a spiritual vacuum, for its myths and images have been called irrational *simulacra,* fantasies of fear and desire. The end is depression—and this suggests that the pervading, though masked, depression in our civilization is partly a response of the soul to its lost underworld.

(73–74)

The Mexican materials were gathered from his summers in Mexico, after which he returned to Bloomington to resume study; the Asian scenes came from his experience teaching in Taiwan in the Far East program of the University of Maryland, which staffs military education programs abroad. After his stint in Taiwan, he moved to Kyoto in 1962 where he finished writing the book. His instincts in making such a work are promising: he had covered two of the centers of postmodern interest—Mexico, with its Indian heritage and long history as a degraded colony of Spain, and Japan as a source of philosophical alternatives to Western thought, the wisdom of a culture defeated in the last war. The poems are adequate if not remarkable as chronicle. The only significant innovation is in how Eshleman shuffles together his poems, merging his experience in both places into one emotion. The two cultures are distinguished only by embedded details, not by categorical signs or logical separations. The traveller seems to confer on his images of women the mystery of primal motherhood, the aura of female power, whose roots lay deep in the mythology of the goddess. In "La Mujer," he finds a hut with men and women in a drunken celebration, and he describes one woman thus:

> jammed against broken
> dog-teeth, twisting
> bare-foot on top another
> thighs violently shaking
> & lurching back to bang
> cupboard spilling
> rum, baby-trinkets
> head cleaved open
> from her heels her womb her chest
> song came   *Que boni-*
> *to cielo*
> *Que boni-*
> *ta tierra*
> on her top foot a

           cockroach paused, head
           of spike, visible
           axis of this world

The poems mark a pilgrimage toward an increasingly
fertile landscape, at the center of which is woman; around
her are children, insects, flowers, thick, humid air, the ancient hills, a suffocating scene of the life force in full array.
They end in his "Prothalamion," a long, rambling hymn to
love that celebrates his marriage to Barbara Novak in
Logansport, Indiana, 1961. The various landscapes in the
poems explore a common theme—the poet's repressed sexuality. The image of the wall stands for many things in this
and subsequent books—divided self, polarized world, I and
Thou. "Evocation I" works out a sketch of the wall on which
he tries out some of his newly learned effects:

              I walk a fury
        of gnats, sun tossing on lake-wall
              Mexican dawn burns sorceress across
        waters, circling round me, rising & falling
        whipping her veils of menstruated linens
              odor of earth, damp hay . . .

The wall occurs nine times in the book, each suggesting a
barrier holding back the walker. It is not something to be
surmounted, as it will be later, but ominous and hazy in
meaning. Other repeating images are of encirclings, rooms,
houses, gardens, all ruling off the outside and offering either
shelter or cramped, stifling limits. At one point, he aches
for the liberating violence of the female:

           let her clap my skull-mouth
           open let
           eye see in a severed throat seeds
           taken by harvesting winds

              ("Son of Lightning," *MN*)

The "other" world of Mexico is a vast reality of sexual, mythic, archetypal and esthetic forces that broke through a psychological wall, revealing a vast unknown that had formed the imaginations of Neruda, Vallejo and Borges, even if he recoils from its depths. The young man who speaks in his early poems is still whole and unbreached in intellect; he can take his glimpses into the new dimension of life without trembling. But by the publication of *Indiana* (1969), his first full-length collection of poems, Eshleman had undergone a reversal, a second birth recorded dramatically in the poems. The marriage to Barbara Novak celebrated in the first book becomes the burden of *Indiana*; the birth of a son, Matthew, rejoiced over at first, becomes a crisis later on. All the lines of development leading to conventional middle class life are disrupted in *Indiana*; the old self is rejected, thrown out of the poetry, as a bold new voice takes over. Experience that was once scrutinized dispassionately as an "otherness" of sexually alien content is now a food on which the new self will be nourished. Estrangement, detachment, the categorical reality of that earlier mind are driven from the psyche; and with them must go the wife and child of the first life—they are the steps of an error, a blunder encouraged by all the forces surrounding the youth of the poet—parents, city , education, cultural inheritance. Where other poets might compress their periods of disillusionment into a few short poems of reminiscence, Eshleman makes the struggle between his rival personalities a drama in four acts, each covering a year or two of the psychological transformation he undergoes.

Indiana is a verse chronicle, a kind of "bildungsroman" in which a poet does not simply mature into an artist but takes his former self aside, ritually murders it, then gathers up the parts to recreate himself. The ambiguity of the ritual is necessary: the rite purges him of a self he was given, made into, which he has lugged around into adulthood. It is this old persona he eviscerates; in his belly lives the unborn "other," the twin, the new self whom society did not permit to come to fruition. Once again Eshleman has slipped a second text into his plot: in bringing himself to life out of his own gut, he serves as both midwife and "mother" to his own spirit, a curious rite in which female duties and acts are doubled up on the male figure they work on. What comes out of his own gut in "The Book of Yorunomado," where this ritual occurs, is the stunted and blocked instinctual male who might still possess that set of sexual balances which his society usually cleaves in half to make a man. The embryonic soul lifted out of his smoking wound is the spirit-child that lived all those years in a dark realm of the lower body, in an emotional underworld, the very sort of imp he ran across in the villages of *Mexico & North*. Born out of his own viscera is a kind of Third World native son, a raw material representing a core of energies and instinct still uncorrupted by society. No one in Eshleman's canon goes unscathed by the adult world of polarity and fear; this new baby-self is still blameless passion and vitality, the chief emblem of mid-century idealism.

> I saw I had reached the deadend, but Japan
> was no help, until I also saw
> in the ancient rite of seppuku
> a way. On the pebbles I lowered down
> stonelike. Whereupon the false-Vallejo
> raised before me: cowled, in black robes,
> stern on the roka, raised, he lowered,
> raising a white hand, with his fan he
>
> pointed at my gut; he gave no quarter;
> I cut. Eyes of father, tubes of mother
> swam acid in my eyes red amber
> haze swiftly as one delves through raw

tun with shooting contortions not
moving a foot on the bleeding
pebbles I faced the man I faced the woman
I cored.

(I 21–22)

After evisceration, he remarks, "Goodbye all I've ever known," thus bidding farewell to a former self, and its passive role in life: "I saw nothing as indifference." Using Blake's psychological schema, the old self was an abstraction, an illusory division of light and dark, day and night. Now, however, the evisceration ritual spills blood and sets the contraries of body and soul into a whorl:

for this was the point upon which the knife
twisted

       my contraries
frozen, the blank
zero with a rim,
the navel, the I
has nothing

       set in motion

(I 22–23)

This confrontation between selves, and between Eshleman and his elusive poet/mentor, Vallejo, occurs in a Kyoto coffeeshop with the Japanese name Yorunomado, "night window." It was through a window of the coffeeshop that he looks down to the patio where his ritual re-birth takes place. He had been struggling for some months to translate Vallejo's *Poemas humanos*—but his state of mind prevented him from rendering the imagination of the Peruvian poet until his visceral self-delivery. Vallejo had "impregnated" the poet with an embryonic new self that could succeed in making the translation, but it must be let out before the deadlocked manuscript could be resumed. Hence, Vallejo's surly ghost taunts him at his labor pains, and various false images of Vallejo rise up out of Eshleman's fever. As the new self is born, however, "Vallejo kept his word: He was none other that year than himself."

The "wall" appears again in this poem, and will remain one of the dominant motifs of subsequent books. Other motifs are the caterpillar and its metamorphic counterpart, the butterfly. The wall holds back a flood of merging contents: the caterpillar as a self-transforming insect becomes Eshleman's personal emblem. The insect world in general is his glimpse into the hidden order of nature. Another motif is that of the red spider, with its mythic roots in Arachne, and its suggestion to the poet of a female spirit leading him to the making of his own web of meaning. The spider appears in *The House of Okumura* as the muse of his back garden, and again in his commentary in *Coils;* after she leaves her web, she persists in his memory as a "figure of disembowelment," his own, the post-*seppuku* self he has put at the center of his new poetry.

The act of self-creation in art makes a male's powers of imagination equal to a female's powers of life-bearing. The richer his art, the deeper he draws from his own feminine energy, and he will no longer crave females as his sexual prey. Eshleman's theory of sexuality goes something like this: the average male is shorn of his femininity early in youth and is raised as a hypermasculinized opposite of women. His sensitivities are blunted and he grows up long-ing for his own internal counterpart which he comes to believe women have taken from him and now teasingly with-hold. He must wrest the missing dimension of his soul, the part of himself stolen by society, from women by seduction, even rape if necessary, or by the crudities of conventional marriage and its polarized sexual relations. Intercourse acts as a kind of theft, a momentary repossession of one's missing femininity gotten by a form of burglary, a forced entry and devouring of the feminine spirit. It is only when the male rediscovers his own feminine side within by art or by sexual therapy that he restores the balance in which intercourse is no longer a theft but a mystery to be shared with a lover. Now that he has "darkened the light," that is, crossed the female power of darkness with the masculine powers of light, he perceives his wife without passion. He wishes only to disburden himself of the convention of marriage to his "opposite." She no longer holds him by her sexual attraction, which overwhelmed him so long as he was uncreative. The "escape" from Barbara, and subsequently from their son Matthew, replays the drama of the escaping ego from the great unconsciousness, the womb of darkness Jung describes in *Symbols of Transformation* (which Eshleman had read in Kyoto in 1963) and which Erich Neumann recounts in *The Origins and History of Consciousness*. Eshleman is only vaguely aware of these mythic connections to his crisis; rather, he describes a certain revulsion for a wife he created from hunger. She is attached to the self he discarded, and must be rejected as well. In later sections of *Indiana*, however, he rediscovers the female as an autonomous force, as a collaborator in sexual experience, not as an object to be acted upon for satisfaction. After his marriage to Caryl Reiter in 1970, there begins Eshleman's sense that a woman/wife is the collaborator in his artistic creativity as well. But these maturing attitudes to women take time, and are secondary to a desire to nurture the creative powers of the new self of "The Book of Yorunomado."

The idea of the self-creating act fascinates Eshleman in his later poetry; it stands for something more than his own delivery from an "Indiana, Presbyterian ego," that "big band" he had snapped off, to use a Reichian image. The imagination is a faculty which abstracts a portion of self into an image, and thus isolates qualities of self to be idealized. A poem digs under the political surface of idealization to reconnoiter in the psychic underworld and pull up the buried life that civilization rejects. The thing one made through his imaginative labors was all-revealing of the maker. That is why Eshleman doubles the image of the poem as birth and revelation, for its function as writing is to bring to a surface some gestating version of self. His later poetry will argue a thesis that uncreative nations plunder others in search of that desired "femininity" which they had destroyed in themselves. This later political allegory develops directly out of the musings of "The Book of Yorunomado"—that the origins of civilization itself, of human identity, spring from the first instance of a life-form in effigy daubed onto a cave wall in the paleolithic era. This is the first such birthing of self out of primordial darkness, which Eshleman reenacts in "Visions of the Fathers of Lascaux." The act of such imaging onto a cave wall begins the separation of man from nature, of light from dark. The image was a lifeless outline, and it was put onto a rock wall that limned the first of many impediments set up between the mind and the realms of natural interaction. The birth of a primordial image would spawn the endless generations of alienated man, of abstraction, of etiolated life.

> then the Fathers sucked his brains
> tasting the visionary prisoner raised from the lower
>   body to a skull enwalled garden—
> adders flickering from their ears, they heard cock
> separate from Savolathersilonigh
> the wall of language, it was the truth
> but the truth had to be spread as skin, as target,
> the Fathers had to spot the cave shapes that suggested
>   an animal in absence

(F 71)

In his mature work, Eshleman has been arguing the notion of art as a working backward toward the primal image, in an effort to undo the errors that have accumulated from it. The purpose of the poem now, as demonstrated in recent work, is to regain the primordial opportunity—the glimpse of human innocence in the natural realm. The poem must work in the abstract orders of language, in image-making, but not to increase the distance from nature; rather, the poem must regress into the dark of its own origins, and create selves that are less and less defined by precept and rule. The first birth was a sorting out of human identity, which began the quest for "light"; "The Book of Yorunomado" is a rebirth of self through a night window, in a "darkening of the light."

Coils, issued by Black Sparrow in 1973, Eshleman's journal of poems and commentary covering the same years as *Indiana,* contains other versions of some poems in *Indiana.* The first section is devoted to his "rebirth" in the Yorunomado coffee house in Kyoto. "Webs of Entry," the opening poem, is actually an ur-version of "The Book of Yorunomado," accompanied by a prose introduction to the section. The draft has less music in it, but there are more signs posted as to the thematic intent: a quote from Vallejo is interjected:

> *You, then, have been born; that*
> *too is too obvious, luckless and shut up*
> *and stand the street fate gave you*

Of his stalled effort to translate Vallejo, he says in his introduction to section one:

> I was struggling with a man more than with a text, and that this struggle was a matter of my becoming or failing to become a poet. The man I was struggling with not only did not want his words changed from one language to another, but it seemed as if he did not want

to be changed himself. I began to realize that in working on Vallejo I had ceased merely to be what I was before coming to Japan, that I had a glimpse now of another life, a life that I was to create rather than be given, and this other man I was struggling with was the old Clayton who was resisting change. The old Clayton wanted to continue living in his white Indiana Protestant world of "light"—not really light, but the "light" of man associated with day/clarity/good . . . The darkness that was beginning to make itself felt in my sensibility could be viewed as the breaking up of that "light."

(C 10)

And in "The Library," later in section one of *Indiana,* he remarks,

> Either masturbate or sleep—
> that's how it was translating Vallejo those days,
>
> . . . I ached.
> & Vallejo lay mute.

(I 28)

Olson is another source of self-transforming powers and his presence in the later poems of section one is pronounced. Olson's metaphor of the bird's nest in "The Kingfishers" as a creative circle representing the mind's shaping powers, is applied directly to Eshleman's struggles as an emerging poet in "Nestual Investigations." The kingfisher's nest is a complex phenomenon for Olson: it shows the bird's instinctual power to form the odds and ends of nature into a useful cup, but also shows that the young are born on the mother's vomit, the corruptions and errors of the past, on which they are nourished. Eshleman takes both views in his own "investigations," as he claims the mantle of poet for himself and complains against the delusions and

misjudgments of his midwest rearing, especially as he recalls
a lurid seduction in his youth when he debased the female
in himself and the girl he seduced. The situation of the poem
occurs in Kyoto, as he drives with Barbara along a country
road and retrieves a bird's nest and brings it to their house.
It operates upon his emotions as a powerful vortex—recalling
his youthful intransigence and misconceptions, his own
desultory relation to Barbara, and his thwarted efforts "To
contemplate my sex without disgust." The nest, he tells us,
"is built above the swamp," and his escape from his past
lies in facing the erotic without fear or trembling. "Thank
god hell is not dead in me," he says, and then, "I look at
my filthy hands," which bear the marks of a descent. You
must "lose your life to be a man," and "lose your father to
be a sun," derived from Olson, who argued the same points
in *Call Me Ishmael.* Olson called those who did not challenge
their fathers the enceladic ones, cowards who forfeited their
adulthood. This and the concluding poem "The White Tiger"
retrace the theme of self-birth and reinforce the claim of
a newly-earned poetic power. "Character" Eshleman defines
as "faith in labor," a faith in his own creativity. Using Olson's
terminology, Eshleman remarks that before his rebirth "the
poem wld not forward." Both Duncan and Olson have their
influences on this poem: Duncan's tiger of imagination
prowls the flaming landscape of this agonized lyric; earlier,
Eshleman warns us that "the imagination rejects even the
most filthy matter to its peril."

> . . . getting from being a middle-class youth in a frater-
> nity with a convertible to an artistic consciousness is
> difficult enough that I always fear I will risk writing
> *about* that threshold, centering my writing on the
> doorstep and not passing thru . . .
> . . . at the center of any artist's life (by which of course
> I mean writing/living) is his relation to other men &

women, his sex life at large . . . all my poetry to date
[is] a kind of inferno chasing its own penis.

("Letter to César Calvo," I 55)

The emblematic gesture of part one of *Indiana*—the eviscerating birth—has no counterpart in succeeding sections. The nurturing of a second self puzzles and frustrates Eshleman, who confesses to the young Peruvian poet César Calvo his fear that he may have become stalled on the theme of rebirth without moving forward to the vision of his new sensibility. Part two, which records his sojourn in Lima, Peru, in 1965, when he was working on his translation of Vallejo's *Poemas humanos,* concludes with his first months in New York after separating from Barbara. The underlying tension of the poems is between his poetic convictions, which dictate his separation and pursuit of a new relation with women, and the bonds of domesticity, strengthened by the birth of his son Matthew in the spring of 1965. The translations of Vallejo draw the new identity out of Eshleman, who finds his efforts succeeding at last in rendering an authentic voice for the Peruvian poet—quickening his transformation as he proceeds. Nothing else could verify his own change than to bring to English the intractable complexity and earthiness of Vallejo—even as his "old" self becomes rooted in fatherhood and marriage.

Eshleman's predicament is rich in American content—the theme of artistic integrity versus domestic compliance has been treated countless way in the centuries of American writing. Domesticity is usually viewed as a dilution of powers in the male: his compromise with himself makes possible his duties and obligations as provider. The formative years of the nation may have provoked the issue—since much of a male's activity in wilderness was with his own sex, laying the foundation for a mystique of masculine prowess in which marriage came to be equated with settlement and loss of autonomy, and by consequence, loss of wilderness adventure. The polarity of the sexes seems to have developed slowly as the experience of wilderness and settlement repeated itself throughout the westward migration. By the late nineteenth century, the situation of the sexes in America reached a pitch of separation; the stories and sketches of regional writers of the era point out an excess of spinsters in New England and a concentration of young males in the mining camps of the closing western frontiers. Only the midwest seemed to strike a balance through its peaceful settlement and rapid development of cities—hence, the maligning of the region by many of its native sons, including Eshleman, who have complained in chorus of the drab, uneventful character of their region. The mystique of the male did not diminish in later decades, but grew more subtle and complex: success in business and art seemed to demand a break with domestic bonds, as if the bonds of marriage and parenthood would divert the strength needed to pursue one's goals. Bohemian subcultures have always emphasized either free love between the sexes or homosexual love as alternatives to the threat of debilitating domesticity. Jonathan Katz's *Gay American History* (1976) reprints documents and letters to suggest strongly this pattern of bohemian sexuality, even among the transcendentalists. Black Mountain College came under the sexual scrutiny of Martin Duberman, whose *Black Mountain: An Exploration in Community* (1973) shows that under Olson the school became a male enclave. Many have complained that the movement which developed out of the college is emphatically an art of male experience.

Eshleman's perspective on his own situation derives from Jung: the polarity of the sexes, he argues, led to the polarity of one's own sexuality, forcing men to conceal their innate feminine characteristics and women to annihilate their counterbalancing masculinity. Hence, individuals are driven to conflict within themselves that then spreads to conflict between each other, making marriage a bond of errors and misperceptions of each other's qualities. He regarded himself as having been raised to develop only his male side, and then to prey upon the simplified anatomical identity of the female, under which delusion of sexuality he entered marriage. He had courted Barbara in the error of his predatory nature, and now, with the emergence of a newly balanced sensibility, Barbara remained fixed at the feminine pole and mocked his efforts to reclaim a full self. There was, apparently, no means for Barbara's own reeducation; Eshleman's efforts are perplexing enough to him that he conducts them in anxious secrecy from his wife, dreading the ultimate consquence in divorce and loss of his son.

Eshleman does not want to invert his propensities and become "female" but to shift his attention from the mind, where psychological polarity of the sexes is rooted, to the body, which contains the balanced proportion of sexual traits. By freeing "the lower body," one frees the imagination for art, hence the emergency of resolving these questions about sexual identity. He tells César Calvo that "young artists in North America" are addressing this conflict of sexual identity within themselves, but the success of their efforts to transcend the dilemma of sexual polarity in American life will " 'turn' on the issue of to what extent 'the body' is resolved" in their art. "The sexual must be cleared as it always shd have been," he remarks, to resolve not only the issues holding back the art of poetry in America, but also the issue of one's happiness in life. Indeed, the sexual issue is only partly an esthetic one; Eshleman tells Calvo that he is aware that Vallejo's *Poemas humanos* are a failure—"a failure to be human without writing." It shows a man "needing to write to be human & never quite making it." Eshleman sides with Olson in seeing the poet as a means for the recovery of freedom for others—that his art will clear the way for living one's life to the full outside it, in the grip of reality. "The sexual must be cleared," Eshleman argues, so that all can "live at the limit of our HUMANITY." Vallejo is found in the act of overcoming his own sexual torment, at which point, Eshleman writes, "I wld hook onto him, . . . hook into *Poemas humanos.*" But Eshleman wants to create a poetry that will restore his humanity outside the poem, in his own personal life.

Already, Eshleman suspects that the sexual issue is the cause of America's conflicts with other nations. He hints in his letter to Calvo that "the war in Vietnam" is a "failure of two men/women to talk, to hear the other out." "North Americans are paying the price for exactly what they suppress." Whitman claimed as much in his own time in his preface to *Leaves of Grass* (1855), arguing that his age lacked a dignifying, clarifying poetry to raise awareness and expand the affections. A century later, a new American poet voiced his alarm that the sexuality of Americans was at such an impasse of communication, individually and collectively, that wars and aggression were stemming from the aridity of its own restrictions. Over the years, this thesis has expanded into an extended critique of America's destruction of Third World countries, which he traces back to a masculinized rationality at war with natural instinct and mystery. Whereas Olson made a connection between poetry and ethics, and Pound joined poetry to political philosophy, Eshleman began a life-long effort to link poetry with sexuality, in some ways the richest and most pervasive influence upon the art. All three regarded the poem as a powerful social tool, and Eshleman clearly hoped that by resolving the sexual conflict in poetry, his generation would clear the way for wider self-examination in the nation. Eshleman's concern with sexuality anticipated by a few years the liberation movements among women and homosexuals in America.

"Letter to César Calvo" anchors the work of section

two of *Indiana*—a mixture of prose and poems devoted to a discussion of his emerging poetic. Two other pieces are crucial to the discussion, Eshleman's prose elegy, "Bud Powell 1925–1966," and the mixed prose and poetry of "Theseus Ariadne." Coursing around these exploratory statements are lyric sequences that seem to test the ideas being raised for discussion. A new voice is tried out in them, particularly in the selected lyrics from a work entitled *Walks*, published by Eshleman's *Caterpillar* press in 1967. Eshleman weaves the sequence in and out of other poems, a technique borrowed from Robert Duncan's similar arrangement of the sequences "The Structure of Rime" and "Passages" throughout *Roots and Branches* (1964) and *Bending the Bow* (1968). "Sensing Duncan" is another two-part sequence in section two, suggesting a deepening interest in Duncan's explorations of the sexually-defined psyche.

Eshleman's letter to Calvo begins by describing his tour of the Larco Hererra museum in Lima with his mother-in-law, who had come to Lima to see her new grandson, Matthew. They are told that a basement gallery contained erotic Incan sculptures, kept there to prevent children from finding them. The sexologist Dr. Kinsey had seen them years before and had told Hererra they were not pornographic, but erotic. Eshleman is infuriated to learn that some of the Mochican artifacts have been hidden away, but Sr. Hererra, a good man who had gathered an important archive, wasn't directly to be blamed. The nation of Peru stood at fault; Eshleman later learns that Vallejo's books were out of print at a time when the government had just erected a monument to Peru's most celebrated poet. Walls of suppression seemed to thrust up everywhere in that country, provoking the discussion of sexuality and repression that follows. But there is something else in Eshleman's view of the erotic statuary—it seemed to stand for an impacted sexuality hidden in the "lower" body as well. "Walk VII" picks up on

the description of these various pieces, which he lovingly
describes in all their peculiarity of vision:

A mummy—
voluptuous hair
tiny teeth—head turned aside
(for dentist drill?)
buried with a brown
bird-bag, wearing sticks, sashes,
many cords & a piece of half-
eaten corn in a little basket
skullmouth open to it.

(*I* 45)

His inventory is long and exacting, as he luxuriates over the
intricately merged identities of animals and humans. These
were grotesque fertility figures, and what strikes Eshleman
at every turn is the consistent principle of mingled natures—
the very opposite of polarity in American life and art.
Mochican art is superior to the death cult of Aztec civilization, for there is "nothing *designed* to kill," even the "maces
. . . smashed wine." Here are metaphors and images taken
from the "lower body," on which the Mochica civilization
had nourished its imagination. There is no counterpoint of
rationality to prevent these fusional statements. The museum is a lost vocabulary of sexual vitality, of the liberated
body. The occasionally grotesque exaggerations are instances
of the fusing language of the body—not the refusing
language of the mind. The figurines dimly suggest to him
the direction of his subsequent poetry—as totems and archetypal fragments of a zone of buried human reality. Their
presence in the basement of the museum is a testament to
the suppressiveness of contemporary life.

Eshleman's elegy, "Bud Powell 1925–1966," a prose
poem that is one long aside to the reader, fits into the sequence of poems that sketch out a poetics of the body.

Powell is the musical genius (and deliverer) in his tradition of rebel artists. All through the commentary Eshleman makes contrasts between his own fledgling musical talents, stunted through 12 years of practice by the metronome, against the musical passions of Powell—who he learns was virtually the same age when Eshleman first heard him play on records. So he is to music what Hart Crane is to poetry—a path finder, a dredger up of the body's own hidden darkness. To organize the meditation and make it work in to the other poems, Eshleman deftly establishes the polarity between himself as the white victim of Presbyterian Indianapolis and Powell as the other, the "fire-thief," a close approximation of Duncan's epithet for Olson, "big fire source." But fire from where? Prometheus stole from the gods, but Powell ransacked underworlds and caves of the lower body: "fucked his mother when he played, his sisters, his brothers and he fucked me, all the way thru my anus thru my eyes" (83). The duality implied by the two portraits—the one of Paul Blackburn, the repressed white artist, the other of Powell, the liberated black artist—is not resolved here, just mulled over. The ancient world (to which the Incan figurines belong) has a way of intervening at the edges of metaphor—a strategic new system of allusion that serves as a shorthand reference to complicated psychological and esthetic assumptions. The left hand (sinister side) of Powell, playing the base notes, roamed the keyboard like a "cripple circumambulating a stupa, [and] when it was needed, shoveled in earth." The left side did the plummeting down into the underside, while the right hand went "off into Niagaras & brooks of intuitive visions." The brook will shortly reappear in the landscape of Butler Woods as the boundary line between nature (Powell's country of passion and deliverance) and the hard, cold world of his father's authority.

Powell fits in to the loose outlines of Eshleman's esthetic in many ways. But a reference to a jazz bar in

Indianapolis, the "Black Orchid," where white youths on dates would go to hear "jazz rock & roll," hints if not outright declares that Powell's energy or rich identity has something to do with the larger world that white culture had driven into exile. Powell's force comes partly from his stature as a descendant of remote colonialized worlds, an archetype of the racial exile who draws from a heritage of alienation and despair, outlawed traditions, as inheritor of Africa's rage and primal awareness. "A man does not swing who has not suffered." Going down to a colored bar in the heart of a white city to hear jazz is tantamount to dreaming, and was the only form of "descent" to which Eshleman had access as a teenager. The bar was akin to the woods beyond his window, and to the occasional flashes of intuition he felt as a youngster. What these and other details of his memory build up is not so much the momentary freedom he sometimes experienced, but the curious psychic apartheid that ruled his life and emotions in a city of few admissible paradoxes.

"Theseus Ariadne" completes the three-pronged argument on his new poetics of the body. Eshleman portrays Ariadne as a spider-goddess whose thread is a set of psychological clues by which Theseus is able to explore the labyrinth of *himself*, his own lower body, instead of the usual mythical telling where he merely escapes back to the light. Ariadne forms a partial anagram for Adrienne, Eshleman's lover in New York; their sexual encounters spun him a figurative length of cord by means of which to lower himself down into his own psychological maze. In *Coils*, whose commentaries parallel these lyrics of *Indiana*, Eshleman tells us that after his first night with Adrienne Winograd, he found her in the kitchen taking a bath. He asked her what she did when she was without a lover, and she responded simply, "masturbate." Hence, in this poem,

The wisdom of Adrienne can be summed up in
        5 words: It is
alright to masturbate.

She teaches him to think of sex as pleasure, as liberation, and not as the guilty preoccupation he had made of it throughout youth. She is casual, affectionate, sybaritic, and feels her greatest release through intercourse. This refreshing attitude to love seems to pry loose the remaining inhibitions under which Eshleman suffers. He now has weekly sessions of Reichian therapy under the psychiatrist Sidney Handleman, and together the two sides of his sexual training bring the desired result: a feeling of complete freedom with the body. Towards the close of this mixture of prose and lyric in "Theseus Ariadne," Eshleman reminds himself

        To buy some new clothes—to believe my body is
            worth adorning.

His discussion of new attitudes leads him to generate a list of liberating influences, as in his elegy to Bud Powell. These include, as one might expect, Blake's proverbs from "The Marriage of Heaven and Hell," a quote from D. H. Lawrence's *The Man Who Died* ("They are destinies of splendour after all our doom of littleness and meanness and pain"), Adrienne, and now Jung, whose memoirs are quoted from at length. A telling statement from Jung jibes perfectly with Eshleman's thought: "The more the critical reason dominates, the more impoverished life becomes; but the more of the unconsciousness, and the more of myth we are capable of making conscious, the more of life we integrate."

In September, 1966, Eshleman paid his mother a visit in Indianapolis. The meeting went badly; Eshleman remembers having a bitter misunderstanding with her. The last sediment of his youth seems to have been stirred up and ejected from him. He came to her in the frankness of his Reichian cure, prepared to demonstrate the vitality of his

new self. But the memories and pain of his life in that city
were enough to stir up the old trouble, at which, reenacted
in his poem "The 1802 Blake to Butts Letter Variation," he
sees his deliverance from her in mythic form. The Butler
Woods, which he longingly stared into during childhood
vigils at the rear picture window of his father's house,
becomes the setting for his dream narrative. A creek now
separates the free range of life from the groaning entrapments of his parents' ways. "All my poetry," he writes,
"to now":

> a wall through which I've tried
> entrance, but nevertheless a wall
> Book thrown up to shield me from
> another's sight

> (*I* 89–90)

Troubling him are all the sacrifices deliverance has required.
His wife Barbara and son Matthew have had to be rejected;
his mother now stands in the way of his freedom. These are
costly rejections that he cannot fully justify, even when his
own life is the issue:

> How can you turn from your
> mother's eyes? How can you not
> feel emotion with Barbara?

But Adrienne is a Persephone leading him out of hell:

> I was following her lit taper
> through the sewer of the canal
> but as I touched her gown-strings
> I heard Barbara groan behind
> & Matthew wailing in a cloud
> & my mother set her foot against
> the canal & start to cross
> & my father a winged-ant begging in his own house

And his liberation comes by pulling out the dead matter
blocking the psychological channels to freedom:

> I opened my breast full of maggots
> & as I began to pull them out
> a stench of piss & dust
> blinded my eyes

He walks beyond their reach, across the meadow, following his new muse Persephone, who lives seasonally in both
extremes of the body: summer in light, winter in darkness.
He realizes at the poem's close his gain, finally:

> O God, why has it taken me 31,000 years
> to stand at the threshold
> Why has it taken me 31,000 years to leave home?

(I 92)

The rupture between mother and son during his visit home
provokes perhaps the most startling image of his liberation
and self-making, which forms the epigraph to *Indiana*:

> *Today I have set my crowbar against all I know*
> *In a shower of soot & blood*
> *Breaking the backbone of my mother.*

It is dated 11 September 1966, the date of "The 1802 Blake
to Butts Letter Variation" as well. Gladys Maine Eshleman
was rejected and here dismembered in the violence of his
own rebirth. A reconciliation of profound tenderness will
follow this ritual murder in *Coils*, where he also records all
of this upheaval, but dedicates the book to her, calling her
"my first source of power."

Indiana's last two sections cover the years 1967 and
1968, and contain carefully arranged poems focusing on a
reinterpretation of his sexual youth and on his mature sexuality in 1968. These poems explore the psychic terrain
opened by the Reichian therapy described in the earlier

sections. The poems focus on the riddles of his childhood attitudes, those moments in which his curiosity froze into sexual fear. In the closing section, Eshleman reexamines his attempts to accept women as equals and psychological counterparts, and in a parallel course, begins exploring the mythological content of the "lower body," the underworld within one's self. These explorations of the traumatized psyche ally him with other visionaries of the "dark" side, with Artaud, Duncan, Lawrence, the mature Blake, whose allegorizing of psychic conflicts gives Eshleman a key to dramatizing his own struggles against polarity. Chaim Soutine's paintings are a new source of metaphors for illuminating the unconscious where things merge, remain fluid in identity, and exist as shadowy figures at the borders of life and death. Soutine is the opposite of his father—a sympathetic observer of flesh turning into soul and not flesh turning into a commodity. Soutine's expressionistic depictions of beef carcasses and hanging fowl is a threshold into the nightworld, where life is partially returned to death, a portrait of materiality turning into image. Decomposition is the key to image-making; the objects of waking life undergo a deformation of their identity in the unconscious imagination, as borders, outlines, strict facticity melt away and the underlying, concealed souls of things rise through the decay. Death is thus elemental to the imagination. Hence, Eshleman's fascination with the carefully composed portraits of flayed rabbits, of fish curled neatly into a circle on a plate, of things partially transformed from life to death, in which their essences seem suddenly more vital and exposed. The same may be said for the processes of Eshleman's own image-making lyrics, in which the day world submits to the deformations of humor and derision, of satiric hyperbole and lyric bombast, before the facts of conscious attention can be cooked down into imaginal language. The distortion of reality has freed experience to be ensouled, united, resensualized in lyrical language.

The haunting theme of part two, the loss of wife and son, reappears in the section "1967," especially in the poem "The Yellow Garment," the discarded covering over the soul, where he remarks,

> I must risk bringing myself
> —knowing that what is complete cannot endure—
> to completion by
> myself
>   alone.

The contradiction implied here between the perishable completeness of things and the completing of oneself is resolvable in this context: tearing down "complete" experience, information that has turned into "frozen" categories, allows the self to reunify its sensibility, to join the "death" and "life" of consciousness into a single form.

In a dreamy address to Barbara, Eshleman says, "You were the girl / I chose, Who wanted to serve / & still do / & who I have now pushed / bowl / away from my hand." The effect of this and other returns to the theme of his rejection of wife and child renders his self-making into poet a difficult quest, requiring endless farewells and fond looks backward to home and hearth.

The second half of *Indiana* is a poetry being pulled out of traditional shape; at times the language is tortured into oblique syntactical structures or halted by sudden interruptions of raw sexual content. The poems are overtaken by sudden rushes of unrepressed memory, as the Reichian therapy emboldens Eshleman to "snap the bands" of his emotional constraints. The poems begin by building up frail structures, tentative beginnings of argument, or raw desire. "The Bank" of section three of *Indiana* is a good instance of the distressed language of the new style. It opens breathlessly in the middle of thought:

a man
  killed,
 buried
in the bank, topknot
of the force
from wch wave creepers
vines
ants
crawl over pebbles,

(*I* 112)

The language gives us clots of information lifted out of what
are many converging lines of thought. Only a core of subject matter is presented, quickly, without typographical conventions. It resembles a hastily jotted note; in fact, haste
is its main expression, a gasped report that is forced into
speech among other emergency consideration. But there is
no identity to the dead figure nor any relation established
thus far. There is only, to the clever reader, a dim notion
of connection between this instance and something
remarked in the "Letter to César Calvo" having to do with
another "bank"—

> here I must turn again to Vallejo, as I think you must,
> & face what seems to me the total absence of what Rilke
> speaks of in the *Human Poems*. For the world to come
> through, man must make himself transparent & I
> believe (for I must respond to Rilke or to quote him is
> unjust) that the "mildness" is the seeing of oneself,
> one's organ, as part of a bank tangled with trees &
> flowers, wrestling perhaps as men in a river.

(*I* 63)

On the canal in the dreamscape of "The 1802 Blake to Butts
Letter Variation," the water separates two distinct stages

of life for Eshleman. Thus, it is the transfigured, psychologically rich *place* that makes the dead figure already important—he has sunk into the archetypal realm and radiates its meaning, "the topknot" among its symbolic vegetations. Here is the freedom point in Eshleman's musings thus far, where a "figure," as yet unidentified, but clearly like himself, has sunk down into it—like a character in an expressionistic play staggering to some emblematic setting which speaks *for* him. No sooner is this felt than the "meaning" is blurted forth:

> this night
> I have grasped my life
> is absolute contradiction
> he seeds me
> this man
> buried in the force,

The "force" is the psychological landscape itself. The emergency is a bold new perception, the "absolute contradiction" which the death of this figure has revealed. We know nothing else from the poem except that this figure lies in the mode of a "transparent life" on the tangled bank. This alone tells us, however, that he is given over altogether to the natural realm, a figure utterly transformed and returned to nature:

> he is buried
> obliquely
> in the herd,
> this hump of absolute muscle
> Che Guevara
> from wch wave creepers
> wine
> all harvests so pinioned upon him

The passage rephrases the core of Olson's own vision, stated forcefully in his *The Special View of History* (1970):

> In the end, when all the estrangement is over, when the familiar is known, who isn't up against the face of God like a wall or a mirror where the shadow or the cut-out shape or the light is in the reflection or the light or the figure of himself in species?

> (26)

The figure of Che Guevara is the nearly transubstantiated human of postmodernist ideology, and Eshleman's poem has received the figure into its own prepared psychological realm. The "absolute contradiction" may now be fully stated, for the other half of the poem moves jerkily into a fragmentary portrait of the poet's father, the efficiency engineer at his post in the slaughterhouse, making up the charts of his "time-and-motion" study. He is at the other pole of the ideal—the hyperrationalized middle class functionary, whose work is at the altars of animal destruction, as he oversees the drudgery of black laborers. His white lab frock makes an icy metaphor of the sort of distance and delusion in which the scientific middle class now conducts its affairs:

> Next to the slaughterhouse
> in a radiator of white iron
> Next to it
> he wrote
>
> Next to the slaughterhouse
> in a radiator of white iron
> he wrote
> he wore home

    with chips of steel
    with the tail soaked strawberry red
    he wrote Black Men
    in a ledger he wore home

    he wrote Black Men
    8 can do it in an hour
    with chips of steel
    with his tail soaked strawberry red

    he wrote Slaughterhouse
    he showed no one
    he meant the gate opens only in
    he said God didn't mean us to mate with Negroes . . .

(I 112–113)

All the impediments to speech of a child's repressed attitude
are present in the language—the restarted sentence with its
hesitant beginning "Next," the layered narrative that proceeds without transition, piling up emotional emblems—
"chips of steel," "Black Men," the eerie hell-door of the
slaughter traps opening "only in."

The poem gives two portraits of men against each
other, in which the young poet is the embattled third party
trying to find synthesis between them. The third movement
of the poem concludes the argument with his own portrait—
caught between two forces, arguing against his father's op-
pressive authority:

    this is why you sat on the back porch at nine
    & argued & argued, even then
    wasn't he dead in you

The father slaughters; the natural figure in the tangled bank
was slaughtered. The forces are a culture of death against a
culture of liberation. The father is then described as "tangled

113

in his mind," whereas Guevara is in the entanglements of nature.

The preceding poem, "New Guinea," based on a *National Geographic* photograph of four headhunters on a log which he remembers seeing in early youth, sets the tone for the poems that follow. However blunt and terrifying the life of those men may seem, he now feels "entered by the ghost / / O primavera tuberosa," the savage spirit that inheres in the tribe. He has been pushed to the side of primal nature, which allows him to reject what his father stood for in "The Bank." And in "The Creek" which follows, the bank reappears in new guise—a tangled bank seen from the *benjo* (outhouse) window at Will Petersen's house in Kyoto—

> a bank tangled wildflowers stringers
> lean wrestlers agrapple trees
> diagonal shot
> lazy with goldfish
> black churn of the source
> carrying away my eternity under me

> (*I* 115)

The overlaying of fragments of different narratives reaches a new density in this and succeeding poems—the point of juxtaposing and overlaying various stories to have a single archetype emerge from among them. The model of thought proposed by the poem is of a mind threading its way into the emotional past by means of associations, fragments of riming memories that form a circuit or pathway to the source of trauma, where recollection ceases and perception or resolution takes over—bringing us back to the present by the same route. The mind is a landscape of thickets and tangled paths strewn with the ruins of past experience by which one traces a narrative of mishaps and disappointments—the "case" histories through which a personality was formed or one's character was sundered. One's own memory "banks," tangled with associations, form a wilderness, perhaps a "third world" within, where primitive thought and desires are more or less colonialized, exploited, suppressed. These narrative recollections are acts of self-discovery, and their processes involve a trek through undergrowth in search of the remains of childhood, as if it were an ancient temple buried under vines or ravaged by social forces. Eshleman's associative recollection is the hallmark of "deep image" poetry; the long strophe-like progress of thinking backwards to traumatic origins defines the mode of Wakoski's poetry as well. Rothenberg's poems since the publication of *Poland 1931* proceed as acts of surrealistic recollection, but the end is identical to Eshleman's: to discover the moment at which the self was severed from its soul. Antin, Schwerner, Owens, and Kelly all pursue a poetry of self-examination by tracing linked associations of memory to emotional origins. Their poetry is an heir to psychoanalysis, and as poets they express the anguished white conscience in the post-imperial age.

"The Bank" moves sinuously through juxtaposing images of creeks and creekbanks drawn from Eshleman's Indianapolis childhood, and from Kyoto, and during a therapy session with Sidney Handelman, as the fusion process works back and forth across the surface of memory. The archetypal event is again the head-on conflict of a culture of destruction and a culture of nature and renewal, with the poet reeling for balance inbetween. Now all layers of the narrative, from across time, begin converging into a pattern as a rambling patient feels areas of mind suddenly unlock. Everything feeds into the central event—the boy's sudden impulse to grapple sexually with the family dog just as his father discovers him, saying once "You shouldn't do that."

The father represents the voice of "injunction / injunction / never an end." He continues his vigil at the edge of his yard, guarding the wildernesss the boy longs to enter. He is a concatenation of laws framing human behavior, a lawgiver of the Old Testament. He is the rational authority of the male sex, voicing its domination over nature at the far end of masculinity. The creek "feeds & feeds" and runs beyond the square of mowed grass his father owns, where the boy tried mating with the dog. The creek is the feminine principle, the fluidity he longs to possess—the stream that suggests instantly a flowing of all the frozen emotion and feeling built up since childhood. The creek is where things mingle and the fusion process begins. Every meadow he can remember slants down to one, and he recalls discerning the dark water amidst his own emotional turmoil—now under Handelman's therapeutic coaching, other times at his vigil at the window, seeing the far off creek behind his house, and from "the Officers' Barracks at the S A C Compound Seoul," the meadow. The word "feeds" begins the poem, but ends a sentence that includes the title, "The Creek." The creek feeds. It nourishes the psyche, whereas the rest of his psychological landscape describes emotional starvation. The boy explains feebly to his father that he "was just playing with Sparkie," who then becomes a woman, and now the creek. Each of these images is a variation of sexual wonder the boy happened upon, and was arrested at by the power of his father.

Fused imagery is raised to another power in "Bear Field." The poem only partly fills in another traumatic episode with the father, another memory he calls up in an effort to unlock himself. It begins in the middle of a thought and narrates a time ("I was 15") he and his father stood off from the car and relieved themselves. His father's penis was *"out of view / out of view,"* but it was the organ that "in the form of an arrow / had manifested himself thru / my mother to me"; he then turns to the boy and asks, "is that your firecracker?" The image of an "arrow point" closing the poem has no meaning until one comes upon the later poem "Diagonal," which finishes the story. The "arrow point" is a road sign marking a curve, but its red point is phallic and paternal, the organ of generation, the totem at the base of all his efforts to change his attitudes. The two poems begin with an incident in Kyoto, but another situation suddenly intervenes from New York, where he remembers walking on "6th Avenue" as a pedestrian signal recalled the Kyoto road sign, the arrow leading back to his father, and finally to the *National Geographic* photograph of headhunters, those assembled males astride their wooden log, their phallic arrow. "I've been at this poem / for centuries," he remarks in "Diagonal," as he steps back and finds himself in a long tradition of poetry, beginning with Blake or even Christopher Smart, in which the sexual issue is raised but not resolved. Man is the "diagonal," the line that suggests the erect phallus; but woman is now assigned her own archetype, the "Circle,"

> I must sense
> ring in the water
> to wholly love
> anyone—
>
> (*I* 143)

The creek, the bank, the circle are all finally worked into a single archetype, a "ring in the water," as a long process of sorting out sexual signs ends with a deep image. The father's yard is bordered with lattice work covered in morning glories, but nonetheless a wooden "wall," preventing the boy from escaping his father's bleak vision of the world to the meadow that reaches out and descends to the creek.

"The Bedford Vision" can now make use of the whole assemblage of motifs by presenting the sexual liberation of a female who figures as Libra having intercourse with Taurus, after which she gains her freedom:

> And I saw her cross
> that curious little stream
> that runs outside the limits of
> the known world,
> for each man
> and each woman such stream is different

(I 147)

Through intercourse, the orgasm, one enters the stream, the "creek" which runs all through these poems on sexual recovery.

Section four opens on a final theme, "what I've escaped is / greatly what's let go of me," in "The Black Hat," which moves sluggishly forward with a burden of criss-crossed subjects and patterns. The poet's father looms in the background; the rejected wife and child are always lurking somewhere in the back of his mind; but Eshleman tells us obliquely that he is rushing to the "Yuk Soo / Chinese Laundry," and not until the end of the poem do we discover that the laundry is a metaphor of the psychological cleansing he accomplished through Reichian therapy. The poem announces the complex mood of liberation and renewal that the remaining poems will flesh out. Yuk Soo offers him a kind of Lethean immersion, where he leaves behind the error and misjudgment he has accumulated: "I'm here / because I left the place / established for me."

The early poetry was fragile and desperate, confined to descriptions of an oddly twisted terrain outside the poet, projected onto landscapes either in Mexico, Taiwan, Korea, Japan, but heaped up in the alien and remote worlds he visited as a stranger. The deeper imagery of emotion sprawled thinly over those terrains and peeked out at him from certain women or the stark, dreary poverty of village streets, or in the rituals he happened upon. As he matured, Eshleman's poetry slowly shifted ground to an inner landscape, where the imagery was now drawn from memory, the reservoirs of personal experience, whose roots dangled down into the unconscious where a deeper imagery connected individual to collective life. The remote and strange suddenly appeared within, as Eshleman discovered the real theater of poetry—the grotesque inner domain which sprawled around in its own buried tropics. The immaculate, stifling atmosphere of the ego was akin to a sort of white capital planted in the rain forests; the poems run out into the dark emotional foliage of memory like so many footpaths we trace as readers, as Eshleman heads in to discover his primitive early likeness living in some apparitional form in the weird half-lit interiors. The more he puts himself into his quests of an ur-self, the primordial youth, the more the elder sloughs his self-consciousness and the orderly intellect of an alienated white citizen. The quest into self and its hiding place in the lived past is itself the ordeal of death and renewal, the rite of passage of an adult who trudges back down the same route he had come up in order to mature. He disappears out of the ruined adult and back into the undivided self that lives somewhere in those paradisal settings Bud Powell evoked on the piano, or Hart Crane imagined in those impassioned lyrics over the Caribbean world. The slaughtered Guevara was returned, dumped perhaps, back into the archetypal setting which his career as a revolutionary had made the counterpoint to corrupt imperialism. What Mao was to China in "The Kingfishers," postmodernism's first anti-imperialist poem, Guevara is to Eshleman; but behind the slaughtered corpse of Guevara in the sacred wood lies the spectral and still-living figure of the poet himself, whom he rescues each time he makes a lyric foray into memory.

Now art can be said to be the "impossible amalgam" ("Soutine"), the absolute engagement of the not-I in which one risks the dissolution of self. The ecstasy of all such streaming forth of emotion is in becoming merged with the rest of life, the all. Therefore,

> I cannot see

> a flower without
> facing myself
> stript of time . . .

> (*I* 161)

> I cannot watch a stone move

> but I know we're becoming a star
> shower

> (*I* 163)

Even to touch his son Matthew "is to / enter a cathe- / / dral, I mean / awe." Such comparisons between the elastic self and the immensity of life come down to us throughout the whole visionary tradition from Blake to Olson. But in Whitman alone one finds numerous such comparisons— "elbows in sea gaps," the "orchard of stars"—within his grasp, and in Pound the feeling of "timelessness" when Image seizes the mind. The ecstasy of merging with the All dissolves his jealous possession of the female, for each sex houses a spirit in a "wayward form": "I desire her spirit to / be free—this is my love / for her, this is how / my spirit converses with hers" (*I* 47).

Eshleman reserves two important poems to close the winding argument of *Indiana*: a meditation on Paul Blackburn and his homage to Chaim Soutine. "Sunday Afternoon" compares the view of the Hudson River from Blackburn's window to the long vigils at his Indianapolis window—both having a common ingredient in the poet's longing for that "rock majesty tree greenery" below. He knows he is composed of contradictory attitudes: a "sickness walking past . . . the bar in Sunday" and

yet in the same wink of eternity
God in the light shafting down Mercer
man free
drunk in the ecstasy of his juices

(I 166)

This was the same paradox he felt when very young, when
he went to his window

as to a kind of lip of life
as a man comes to a place & touches it
wants very naturally to enter it

(I 167)

where children played on the lawn across the street, the sons
of a divorced Catholic father who now had a girlfriend. His
own father could only scorn the openness of Mr. Kirk's
affections:

my father commenting over supper
(this is such an old story Paul)
shameful how they act that way all the neighbors
can see
& I agreeing, my mother's face coming rigid
mouth setting looking at my father

who, upon recollection, the poet says was

Death reading the funnies
with his weird bride, hair up in nightcrawlers
strange antiseptic odors of the bath
both their stomachs constantly upset

And he remembers

standing in that dynamite
brown boyscout shoes short pants
unable to stomach what I had decided was right to live
I learned a capacity for anguish

learned to make a place for it fit it in the hymns
bow my head in the circumflex of grief

wch was the figure my body made it seems
a woman hanged in me
hair knotted in the cords of my heart

(I 168)

In contrast is a "new" self, the primitive spirit released back into thought by the threshings of memory. This "second voice" hides out along the edges of the civilized consciousness like a guerilla fighter, a Viet-Cong, and unless there is open conflict within the mind, the second voice slinks away unfelt. Wholeness of self only comes through the rages and civil strife within, hence

when I am most with it I am closest to disaster

(I 168)

The "fusing / of my materials" is a slow process, but the ecstasy/agony of lyric self-immersion brings up another image of the buried tropics, an inner African world:

as I dance my highly specious dance
making a poem like a giant Congo mask
of the forces in me I would approach to
the sun.

("Sunday Afternoon," I 169)

But Eshleman has another way of describing the courage needed to put oneself in the open of his own traumatic history, thus laying himself bare to inner as well as outer reality—an arena Olson defined at the outset of *The Maximus Poems* as "that which is, . . . call it the next second," the contingent drama of reality which Eshleman rephrases as

when I am happiest I risk meeting the next instant.

"Soutine" bids farewell to the "old rite," the ritual slayings he has performed on himself to free his buried spirit. In closing this chapter on his development, he wishes to begin a new kind of artistry in which things are moved "beyond anguish." Soutine represents another of the crucial artist/rebels who serve as guides on his pilgrimage through the psychic underworld. He calls Soutine "the most powerful painter of our time," and his paintings are vast projections of the inner life which Eshleman reads as murky, cartoon-like narratives on the warfare at the base of the soul. What Soutine reports in his studies of the human physiognomy are, in Eshleman's phrase, "the psyche / of the human / face." In his tribute to Soutine, Eshleman refers to a new ritual, the cannibalizing of other spirits. One consumes the soul of another in a newly literal sense of "tradition," the devouring of the dead ancestors, another way down into the spiritual underworld of imagination. One must reconstruct one's own spirituality by absorbing other souls into imagination. Indeed, the lyric journey of the poems is a search for the fragments of discarded spirit, each fragment of which seems to come along and aid the voice that dares explore the painful details of its mysterious tragedy. But Eshleman insists here and elsewhere that the pure or natural soul lives in the "forests of the night," in a terror-riddled world that consciousness loathes and fears. To get at the soul is to pass through a landscape of tigers and dragons, a primeval place so dreadful that Western religion sealed up its passageways and called it hell. But as Rothenberg remarks in "Vienna Blood," in *New Selected Poems*, the base of human awareness is *communitas*, a "holy terror." Soutine is the opposite of Eshleman's father in presenting a violence that heals one's psychic wounds. The blood and gore of the slaughterhouse merely deepened the psychic wounds of civilization by continuing the injury against the natural realm. His father hid from the killings in his small brick office, the subjectivity that walled him off from "that which is":

> my father worked next to the wall against
> whacked bullhead 30 feet up encased red
> brick accountant

(I 170–171)

The poet "never saw them twist / the neck of my dinner," but this is the violence and fearful experience the soul must grapple with to overcome its dread of death. "I slit my throat into my soup / I eat the breast of Soutine / amalgam / amalgam." The poem is a mosaic of narrative bits depicting the reconstitution of a poet's awareness; the intersections between episodes or traumatic scenes make up a brief story line in which the theme of rebirth is subtly pinpointed and clarified. Eshleman surrounds himself with the figures who aided in his recovery; among them is the Marie whose sexual candor taught him to relish the body and freely indulge himself in physical pleasure. Soutine nurtured the spirit by revealing the underworld at the base of human nature. If he could stare down these forms of dread, he could break the hold of his father in his guise as the mysterious lord of animal slaughter. Like a second father, Soutine brings him back to nature, as the interpreter of slaughter rather than its doer or counter of carcasses. Both Marie and Soutine deliver him spiritually to the grove and entangled creek, the wilderness he now calls by a fused name, "the moistinsplendor," the green world that has been beckoning since childhood, "the childwood."

"Soutine" rounds out a narrative of winding subplots and motif-laden vistas, ending a soul's progress toward wholeness and emotional relief. Perhaps the closing portrait of Soutine, in whose realm lives the vivid memory of a fertility goddess, Marie, serves as the coda to the plot, a summing up of events. The final poem gives us a round of new images to add to the compost heap on which the crocus bud blooms at the opening of *Indiana.* The gist of the book is the escape of a middle class youth from the stifling orthodoxy of his midland upbringing; an ego had been drained off from the sensuality of a young man as he was schooled in the principles of competition, rivalry, a hunger for distinction.

What stands out in Eshleman's argument is his premise that it takes radical and outrageous measures to become normal and psychologically healthy. The accumulated fears of the average person would seem to suggest that the social norm was actually the aberrant extreme. But Paul Goodman had already laid out this brief in *Growing Up Absurd*; Eshleman gives us the lyric equivalent of that vivid indictment of stifled senses and crooked priorities in the rearing of America's young. Eshleman's self-portrait in *Mexico & North* captures a college student gawking at Third World squalor and a few glimpses of lingering primal life; his Candide is stiff, tentative, awkward, but almost from the first line of the book Eshleman establishes his subject as important, familiar, essential—a portrait of the American at mid-century, the average midwesterner in whose soul rests all the certainties of ordinary American faith. Eshleman is, beneath the sway of his lush rhetoric and surreal imagery, a dogged realist intrigued by the actual dreariness of daily life. If one could uproot the fundamentals of one's outlook, others could do it too. And if one soul were properly reconstituted, perhaps the world would begin to come togther again, and life make sense. Eshleman is our guide to rebirth; if *he* can do it, *we* can do it. The reformer is in him, and like Snyder or even Rothenberg in his more preacherly aspects in *Symposium of the Whole,* Eshleman proffers a new gospel, a heartland homily on the world we could achieve if our souls were moistened in the creek, and our hearts enlarged by a truce with nature.

Chapter Three

Fathers and Sons

*My tendency so far seems to be to apologize,
thus to be forever a son. If you are a careful reader,
I imagine that you have suspected that I am a kind
of eternal son eternally at war with an eternal father.
The species that is willing to play the son long after
it has ceased to operate as a son because it suspects
what is merely adult.*

("Satanas," WSM 147)

"Isn't it time you stopped roasting Indiana?"

("The Rancid Moonlight Hotel," WSM 171)

I

Something happened at mid-century that sent American
society reeling over the charms, powers, and mystique of
youth; its attractions as a state of mind and being were so
potent that no part of society could withstand them. The
press jubilated over a trend that seemed universal, dur-
able, and exploitable for its advertisers. The elderly were

rediscovering love in the nursing home; those who could afford it thronged to Florida and California for the resuscitating powers of sun and sea, and to the plastic surgeons who could trim their flesh and give them the semblance of youthfulness. Physical fitness forestalled mid-life bulge among those in their prime; highways began to be dotted with week-end joggers; the gymnasium was no longer the preserve of minorities who practiced boxing, but became deluxe fitness centers for the middle class. The Nixon-Kennedy presidential race of 1960 was, finally, a contest between competing social images, and Kennedy's "youthfulness" won out over Nixon's superior intelligence and swarthy, middle-aged looks. Kennedy was himself a formidable symbol of his times: his bright smile, trim, athletic figure, pretty wife, and cheerful youngsters were the sort of young blood America demanded after the gray, mundane years of Eisenhower. The dour image of the presidency was now reversed with Kennedy's candor and accessibility, with his potent call for a "new frontier," which drew upon the mystique of wilderness and youth in the American imagination. His administration, like Roosevelt's, attracted bright young intellectuals from New England; they came to Washington to curb the paternal excesses of corporate business and to counterbalance greybearded free-enterprise ideology, which had reigned in the post-war years. In film, war heroes predominated; but a new "young rebel" began upstaging the burly, savage prowess of the combat idol, whose enemies were parents and a dottering social structure that hemmed in his or her youthful passions.

Youth symbols were everywhere; advertisers described their wares as daring, fresh, and wild; new products coming on the market had sex appeal, charm, zest, zing, were jazzy, sparkling, provocative, exciting, chased away wrinkles and mid-life blues. Madison Avenue used such terms to sell America a dose of rejuvenation on radio, in film shorts, on television, in the magazines and newspapers. It would have been an unthinkable gaffe to apply any of the old prejudices about youth's naivete or greenness or uncouthness to one's merchandise. Detroit would soon catch up to the allures of youthfulness in car design, and offer an array of brightly colored, fantasized sedans with subliminal rocket fins and airplane gun ports. Their body-shapes possessed the suggestive curves and phallic appendages that supposedly aroused the subconscious of potential buyers to "think young" and compelled one to purchase an erotic attention-getter. The automobile was an emblem of free-will, a mechanical reinforcement of autonomy, a symbol of rootlessness and high-energy. All this is made plain in Allen Ginsberg's early poem, "The Green Automobile," written in 1953. A car's perishable newness was itself a metaphor of youth. The more garishly decked in chrome and glittering paint, with a sleek convertible roof of a roomy back seat for love-making, the more richly it became youth's archetype.

In fashion, the long skirt soon rose to middle and then mini length; a more subtle trend was in slacks, some tight-fitting and flattering to a trim figure. But the high-water slacks known as "pedal-pushers," a remake of the old knickers, bore a vent up the sides to reveal a woman's mid-calves, giving her the appearance of having "outgrown" her hand-me-downs. The gamine look of Leslie Caron and Audrey Hepburn was now in; any sort of nonchalance which expressed youth or youthful propensities was fashionable. As a carnival mood overtook the design of casual wear, a drab look was still *de rigueur* for the "adult" male world of business, politics, and the professions. Sober grays and blues belonged to a realm of mid-life activities, whereas leisure and socializing had become linked to the realm of youth.

The destructiveness of war had much to do with the obsession with youth in the post-war era. Revelations of war-time atrocities in Europe and Asia had chilling effects on a population just getting its bearings in the peace years. The menace of atomic war, made real when the Soviets tested their own "nuclear device" in 1949, brought to an end American's brief nuclear monopoly. Now the world stood divided between equally armed and ferocious adversaries. The terrors of war and global holocaust added their burdens to an older population whose lives were measured in depressions, world wars, and now a cold war. There was an unavoidable sense of guilt and failure associated with age: for all of its limitations and frailties, youth was blameless and free to invent a better scheme of things.

Though an eccentric book, Reich's *The Mass Psychology of Fascism* (1946) is a prophetic vision of the social upheavals to come. Virtually every major industrial nation of the West groaned through its sexual revolutions and liberation movements, as each wandered through a maze of alternatives toward the "self-regulatory" equivalent of a "sex-economy." Reich's pronouncements are sometimes uncanny predictions of the struggles to follow. In anticipating women's liberation in the United States he remarked:

> Essentially, the idealization and deification of motherhood, which are so flagrantly at variance with the brutality with which the mothers of the toiling masses are actually treated, serve as means of preventing women from gaining a sexual consciousness, of preventing the imposed sexual repression from breaking through and of preventing sexual anxiety and sexual guilt-feelings from losing their hold.
>
> (105)

Here is "sexual politics" outlined long before Kate Millet's book of that title (published in 1970) spelled it out for a new generation. *"Sexually awakened women, affirmed and recognized as such, would mean the complete collapse of the*

130

authoritarian ideology" [Reich's italics]. "Conservative sexual reform has always made the mistake of merely making a slogan of the right of woman to her own body, and not clearly and unmistakably regarding and defending woman as a *sexual* being, at least as much as it regards and defends her as a mother" (105). A quarter century later, Eshleman reiterated Reich's admonitions in his elegy to his mother, "Coils,"

> You are the woman who gave up your dream when I
>   was born
> I was your dream & thus you no longer had one,
>   conned
> by an aggregate of superstition & partriarchal religious
>   malice
> into believing your function in life was generation at
>   the expense
> of human imaginative fulfillment, yet I must
>   understand your giving
> birth to my body as a sacrifice, your nourishing me
>   as forgiveness, . . .

(*C* 141)

Reich underscored the Romantic tradition's critique of the machine age; others had already argued his case in narrower contexts, but Reich was among the first to offer a broadscale program of reform and social renewal in the context of industrial society. In this, Reich seems particularly allied to D. H. Lawrence, whose fiction, rooted in the squalor and depravity of the mining industry of the English Midlands, cast all of its solutions in a return to primal human relations. Lawrence's principles were ultimately clarified in his novel *Women in Love*, drafted during the first world war and published in 1921. In an early scene set strategically in Ursula Brangwen's classroom, Rupert Birkin, modelled on Lawrence, argues with the airily intellectual Hermione

Roddice, who questions him, a school inspector, on his most basic assumptions:

> "Isn't the mind—" she said, with the convulsed movement of her body, "isn't it our death? Doesn't it destroy all our spontaneity, all our instincts? Are not the young people growing up today, really dead before they have a chance to live?"
>
> "Not because they have too much mind, but too little," he said brutally.
>
> "Are you *sure*?" she cried. "It seems to me the reverse. They are overconscious, burdened to death with consciousness."

To which Birkin responds, in Reichian terms: "Imprisoned within a limited, false set of concepts." Here was the "social armoring" Reich later identified as the means by which industrial capitalism had "imprisoned" mass society. When Hermione next asks him, "But do you really *want* sensuality?" Birkin outlined a portion of Reich's subsequent argument with his answer:

> "Yes," he said, "that and nothing else, at this point. It is a fulfillment—the great dark knowledge you can't have in your head—the dark involuntary being. It is death to one's self—but it is the coming into being of another."

The midcentury was a major crossroads of modern Western history; it saw the passing of European empires and the rise of a vast constellation of ex-colonial states whose alliances were to be won by Russia or the U.S., the giant new empires that had risen out of the ashes of the old European hegemony. Writing in 1964 from the U.S. State Department's perspective on the period, David W. Wainhouse observed,

> We are in the midst of the concluding phase of one of the most historic and dramatic developments of our time—the swift dismantling in the time span of one

generation of the Western colonial systems which have developed over five centuries. Most of the remaining colonial powers are striving to find reasonable and equitable solutions to the problems which face the territories and peoples still under their control.

(Remnants of Empire 1)

American government's reaction to the crisis took the form of imperial self-interest, and encouraged the liberation struggles with mixed motives. On the surface, the U.S. championed the cause of decolonization from its position as an eminent ex-colony; but its advocacy was chiefly goaded by the Cold War and open rivalry with Russia and China for protective client states and strategic buffers. "The attacks on Western colonialism by non-Communist states," Wainhouse wrote, "have been supported and aggravated by the Communist powers not in order to emancipate subjugated peoples, of which there are millions in the Soviet empire, but to facilitate the spread of communism" (*Remnants of Empire* 2). Tainted motives on the one side suggested tainted motives on the other, as the race to dominate the emerging states emboldened the aggressions of both superpowers.

> Like the cold war, the struggle between colonialism and nationalism now pervades the entire complex of world politics—not just the United Nations but also the specialized agencies, such as I.L.O., F.A.O., and UNESCO—poisoning the international atmosphere and exacerbating other problems. It has been a source of embitterment in the relations of the United States with several of its allies and thus a divisive force which has helped to undermine the Western alliance. Some NATO allies have held the United States partly responsible for the loss of their possessions, and suspicions have been voiced, not just in Communist propaganda, that behind the talk of anticolonialism and freedom the American

government and American business seek only to replace the European powers in their colonial territories.

(Remnants of Empire 2)

It was the end of the colonial epoch, an age of "colonial revolution" fueled by all parties to the issue—the criticism of sympathetic new states, "Communist propaganda," and the diplomatic rhetoric of the U.S. State Department. It was an age of liberation of cultures previously considered alien to Western ways. But it was inconceivable to Western governments that such cultures could effectively meet the challenges of independence without the support and protection of their old colonial masters. They would be certain prey to the machinations of new empires. These were "child-like" races, infantile in their reasoning and capacities to govern themselves. They were the benighted dregs of world culture, described variously as "underdeveloped," "weak," "backward," a fringe people subject to primitive myths and superstitions, mainly ignorant and easily misguided. In 1960, John Strachey made the argument for Western protectionism succinctly:

> We see now that we cannot just destroy imperialism and put nothing in its place. There must be some relationship between the developed and the underdeveloped, the strong and the weak. The great centers of industry, capital and power cannot possibly cut themselves off from the vast underdeveloped hinterland which comprises by far the greater part of the world. A new relationship between these two worlds must be found.

(Remnants of Empire 7)

The implicit imagery of Western diplomatic rhetoric described a parent-child relationship to the Third World which justified myriad forms of intervention in internal affairs, even to the planned destabilization of governments, the use of puppet regimes, rigged elections, staged *coups d'état,* all of which were the work of imperialism's invisible hands.

As the U.S. federal government made its sometimes bloodless decisions in the U.N. Security Council, or in its Cold War negotiations with clients abroad, it protected its strategies through an unprecedented enforcement of repressive measures at home. Vying with Russia over the new free states required the suppression of so-called "communist sympathy," hence the numerous agencies of Congress and the Executive to silence or punish those who espoused the rights of self-determination of Third World countries. Or worse, those who applied the lessons of the "colonial revolution" to domestic class and race conflicts. The dark era of government surveillance of home life resulted in part from the paradox of government's vision itself: having both to trumpet the cause of self-determination and self-fulfillment as articles of democratic capitalism while at the same time having to lure free states into the network of its new imperial regime. Buffer states, strategic clients, C.I.A. control of foreign affairs were all aspects of a vulnerable diplomatic strategy whose enemies and critics were forcibly disenfranchised by congressional means. Hence, the dual nature of the 1950s: as an era of repression and regimentation in the domestic social sphere, and as the crucible from which would come profound transformations of the arts and of American esthetics. As federal government and business hardened their approaches to newly decolonized states, American culture explored its sympathies with and alliances to the very "otherness" of the emerging cultures. But cast over the poetry, fiction, drama, dance, theater, and music of the era was a protective subjectivity and obliqueness of manner that made them almost invulnerable to congressional accusation. As Hollywood and the universities came under government scrutiny for explicit violations of loyalty, the other arts proposed far more radical and dangerous propositions in modes that rendered their opinions and attitudes unexcerptable or beyond the grasp of indictable paraphrase. In the plunge to child-like primitive forms, to a "lawlessness" in grammar, syntax, to primal modes of spontaneous execution, uninhibited disclosures, the arts found their response to the age, to its international conflicts, and formed its adversarial stance to federal authoritarianism.

In 1956, Allen Ginsberg's *Howl* sounded all the bases of social complaint at once, from repression, to regimentation, police control, with a disputatiousness that tapped a vast reservoir of alienation among the nation's youths. Ginsberg seemed to prove Hermione's case, for almost at once his poem became a celebrated testament denouncing the destructive designs against youth, not only in the recent war, but now in civilian peace time, as the Cold War accelerated the pace of regimentation in a new race for scientific and technical preeminence. His plea was elementally for the autonomy of the young and the dissident, but it jibed with the sensuous entreaties of another apostle of freedom, Elvis Presley. Youth's leaders, heroes, gurus, and apostles were beginning to emerge in the guise of protest and as trailblazers of social alternatives, some of them pointing away from parental control, Reich's base unit of fascism, and toward sexual freedom, the politics of the "sex-economy."

The conclusion reached by America's post-war painters was that one's personal freedom could no longer be achieved in the contentious arena of class conflicts; neither the left nor the right offered a way out of the "system," which prompted Robert Motherwell, in 1946, to the despairing conclusion that "The future of America is hopeless." It was this very hopelessness that forced the arts backwards, toward a non-committal, disengaged awareness. One's freedom lay in feelings, not in thoughts, in the holistic responsiveness one found in primitive cultures and in the inchoate consciousness of early adolescence. But Motherwell put a limit to the extent of regression possible in the arts by rejecting the example of Breton's surrealism, whose "animal" tendencies and "total surrender to the unconscious" were an absolute disintegration of the psyche. Instead, the retrenchment to a level below the hypertrophied individual consciousness offered the possibility of renewal, of a "rebirth" of awareness as one neared the origin of its powers. This is the point of Serge Guilbaut's assessment of the painters Adolph Gottlieb and Mark Rothko:

> Gottlieb and Rothko believed that myth and primitive art could be used to express contemporary anxieties (though only as a conceptual point of departure, there being little direct formal influence): in 1943 the source of anxiety was the war, in 1946 it was the atomic menace. Their attitude was in itself a myth, the myth of the noble savage, of the return to the womb. They held fast to the notion that with a tabula rasa they could save Western culture, purify it, and rebuild it on new foundations. For them, as we have seen, the political situation had become hopeless in its complexity and absurdity (many who rejected the Marxist left ended up embracing what they had once detested and rallying to the liberal cause).

> (113)

Events in the art world of New York had direct bearing on the beginnings of Eshleman's poetry in Bloomington. When Motherwell observed that "The function of the artist is to express reality as *felt*," he defined feeling as "the response of the 'body and mind' *as a whole* to the events of reality" (80). Like the painters, Rothenberg and Kelly drew the line well before the disintegrative absolute of mere automatism in writing; deep images were to be placed with conscious skill into a resonant continuum to create their effects upon the reader. The composition of a poem, like the making of a picture, required the functions of both sides of mind, rational and irrational, in which to articulate a level of inchoate sensibility before awareness divided into polarized "adult" and "infant" ranges.

In the first half of his career, Eshleman circled round the issue of personal freedom. *Altars* (1971) opens with a problematic self whose plot unfolds with predictable shape: "You have come so far," he writes in "An Ode to Autumn," which begins an excursion around the zodiac, but "repolarization" had set in since the closing triumphs of *Indiana*. The season of fall is linked to the poet's psyche; both are times in which to shed things, and for Eshleman next to be shed was a faulty "personality," the "chaff" of his "34 years." "I 'fell' then," the poem closes, suggesting a "felix culpa" in reverse, a "deconversion." Interestingly, there now appears a form of the Virgin Mary, the astrological figure Virgo, who held up her hand palm outward, in a blocking gesture, as if against him, Eshleman glosses in a note, in a psychedelic poster (reproduced in *Caterpillar* 8/9) as he walked through Greenwich Village one afternoon. She seems to say to him

STOP THE TRAFFIC THAT
THE CHILDREN MAY PASS

The children in this case are those embryonic psyches within one's imperial self, the colonial, unfledged possibilities one could become; the "traffic" is a blur of abstractions and illusions wrought upon him by a false culture, a merely material and highly censored reality of contemporary life. Virgo is a figure of contemplation, a female form who stands out of reach of sexual aggression, who instructs him to stop his life and to let the children "pass," suggesting rebirth.

Psychological changes within the labyrinth of *Altars* occur at various stages of the journey, whenever the extremes or polarities of selfhood are set in motion and become fused under pressure. There is an intriguing glimpse into this process in "Ode to Reich":

Wilhelm, what I am
getting to is to somehow honor the clarification you
gave us of self-sacrifice, that the substance of love is
kept fresh in the death of feminine form, this
   happens in
that meadow, in the giving up of pride & possession, of
man & woman allowing their bodies to convulse, to
   dissolve
truly thoughts & fantasies, this is the sacrifice Blake
   names
Eternal Death, to die there in joy with another, that
   that form
die, that the substance be liberated to find fresh
   form in
creation . . .

(A 72)

Various poems of *Altars* bear the signposts of change in their titles: "The Gates of Capricorn," the dark half-way point "natural to midnight" and "distantly approaching dawn," followed a little later by "The Dissolution," the "thaw, the phase of purgation and martyrdom," what "should be pruned away & forgotten," from which come the most initial sense of rebirth, "infant joy & pain." There follows the "Ode to Reich," and then the "Lustral Waters," the magical "Meadow," the fertile season of spring, and the more violent and profound fusion process of "The Tourbillions," the centrifuge in which the "two ends want to come together," through which "sun and moon" pass equally through the "arch" that a human makes of his life. The outcome of rebirth is cleverly and subtly indicated in the final memory which closes *Altars*: the speaker who began in fall wishing to shed the dead foliage of his life now appears to us in the form of his early recollection, a child between his parents.

139

But the scene shimmers with irreality, and the memory is now a palimpsest of actual events and an overlay of their psychological revisions by the adult recalling them. The mother is advancing upon him menacingly and he is "consumed in her" as he settles "on top of [his father]," who is "writhing now / & blue, & she a gorgeous black exploding fire" (105). The fire is one of final purgation and transformation; out of the magma of the explosion will come a new "form," the one hinted at in "Ode to Reich" which emanates from the death of polarized sexuality, in which parents *and* son dissolve their alienation and become one self. The Maytime of the poem brings a fruitfulness of affections and deeper roots into his personal past. This is "the completeness within the life itself," Eshleman glosses—through the poem alone "can there be a wholeness" which life itself usually forfeits.

Eshleman's early books take the form of epic journeys, quest narratives, in which his drama of self-change and liberation is mythologized. At the outset of *Altars,* Virgo is the goddess who will guide him through the perils of his solar voyage. In a scene of initiation into the "underworld" or maze, in the *Indiana* version of "The Book of Yorunomado (*I* 20), an Ariadne-like "duende" greets him and beckons him toward a sexual depolarization referred to (from the *I Ching*) as "the darkening of the light," the release of one's feminine side into consciousness. In *The Gull Wall,* a guide appears in the opening poem "To the Creative Spirit," another Ariadne figure, the "black spider," his spiritual companion through a four-part voyage of the soul. *Coils* ends at the beginning again, in the poem "Coils," in which the transformed self is told,

> From this point on he [Yorunomado] said,
> your work leads on into the earth.
>
> (*C* 147)

It is different each time the circuit through the lower body or "underworld" is undertaken; each time something new springs from its dormant, alienated state into awareness. In "The Ronin Cock," from *The Gull Wall*, the figure at the end of his journey remarks,

> . . . I would have brought
> the woman I love here, but I knew I had
> to find out what I have and settle with you
> alone.

(*TGW* 111)

Along the way of the journey in *Altars* are familiar apostles of self-transformation, Blake, Reich, and Olson, each of whom offers a counsel of encouragement or wisdom. The voyage around the solar year is a subtler motif than the four-sided plotting of *Indiana*. The circle is both end and beginning, and the rounding of all twelve astrological houses will bring the persona back to where he started, though now changed, a figure transformed. The paradoxes are all intended: sameness in difference, change in repetition, multiplicity in oneness. The astrological circle is emblematic of all the circularities of quest and discovery, and is invested with many symbolic possibilities, including the "circular causation" of the gut, the "soul-center" of the body, where alterations of self are experienced through the act of eating. The circle includes transubstantiation at the sacred altar, the table on which gods die and are reborn, and at which men become gods through ingesting their spirit. All of these things glimmer and dissolve in the fluid textures of this narrative. But all the tributaries of thought lead finally to the *double entendre* of its title: Altars/alters.

Self-recovery, though a limited dramatic concept, possessed a mysterious archetype that is seemingly inexhaustible. One's forays into memory were a trek through an emotional landscape, a rescue operation that possessed keen adventure and intrigue; the self as victim subjectivized the quest and offered a rich potential for imaginary voyages. The "layerings" of abstract expressionist composition, as in deKooning's studies of women where different versions of a woman's portrait are overlaid and partly merged together, as in a palimpsest, suggested the sort of inward journey of recollection in Eshleman's poetry. Pollock's mazes and suspensions of color are maps of an inner landscape, in which various rhythmic patterns compete like thoughts for identity amid myriad other half-patterned activity surrounding, commenting upon, reacting to and enriching these apparitions of meaning. Adulthood was the accumulated foreground static and confusion, the overgrowth and detritus that surrounded the ruins of a sacred realm of youth. Robert Duncan's mental landscapes of the early 1960s, particularly in such poems as "The Song of the Borderguard" and "An Owl Is an Only Bird of Poetry," celebrate the presence of wild youthfulness in the mind, concealed behind reason or adult conscience. This is the stuff of dreams and visions, the magic quality of human nature, which is as furtive as the unicorn. It cannot be captured, and is only, at best, some fleeting emblem of instinctual mystery, the purest sense of freedom that signals its existence the moment it disappears again. In "The Dance," Duncan writes luxuriously of how "our circulations sweeten the meadow," recalling how in "Rubens' riotous scene the May dancers teach us our / learning seeks abandon!"

The rebirth paradigm sweeping across the arts at mid-century was a collective intuition that one's true character lay in the recesses of a youthful prototype, a figure trapped beneath the structures of consciousness. This paradigm brought Frederick Jackson Turner's thesis on the significance of the American frontier to a new stage, in which the frontier, once so real and palpable as a daily experience of Americans, now vanished to become a psychological phantasm, accessible only in dreams, visions, half-formed thoughts and fleeting images. The woods and primal nature were realms of magic, latent with psychological content waiting to be picked apart and reconstituted by succeeding generations.

> I saw the physical world
> a whirlpool whirling out of its flotsam
> spars & wreckage of the golden dream
> man is,
>
> my name is Clayton Eshleman
> was the name given my body at birth
> I am not that body
> I am Yorunomado,
>   cave-scrawler,
>   mocking up
> my original
> renewal of form.

(C 74)

By the 1960s, scientists, long suffering from the reputation of having brought about the Atomic Age, exculpated themselves by voicing from many quarters a new concern for the deterioration of the environment. The new science of ecology became a cause for many younger scientists, whose gloomy prognostications on the state of nature jibed only too well with the general sense of human corruption. Nature's death was predicted variously; Thor Heyerdahl and Jacques Costeau foretold the death of the oceans;

the world's green belt was dying from acid rain; the air was laden with carbon monoxide and other pollutants; fresh waters were toxic around the globe. Wildlife, the concern of numerous societies and organizations, was declining precipitiously, especially in Africa. Nature was described as shrinking, thinning, dying from within, as the encroachments of the human estate accelerated in the 20th century. The theme of youth's recapture thus spilled out of the arts and entered the sciences, where it voiced itself as a gloomy conscience and dark prophecy.

Mid-century society felt claustrophobic and hemmed in by human affairs. It was no longer charmed by the wonders of artificial culture and the mediating functions of bureaucracy. The spread of powerful post-war manufacturing cultures, recently energized by great military campaigns, had enclosed large populations in a controlled reality. Ecology was a form of collectivized conscience, and its language and tropes spread across the Western world, wherever the guilt of modernization demanded a cathartic new science of accusations and atonement. Ecology was the science of guilt and penance, a toter up of the crimes of other sciences. It was staffed in part by maverick scientists who had participated in the overthrow of nature and who now publicly atoned for their acts. The search was on for a means of restoring the original dynamic of man *in* nature, not above or outside it.

How to do so lay with the artists first, whose formulations would search the psychological mazes of rebirth for answers. The rebirth paradigm was a burrowing into the evolutionary past, a return to the source along different pathways of mind and emotion, to reconnect aspects of self thrown off, jettisoned by the forward tide of human history. The modern psyche forced its way upstream, against history, and away from further alienation and entropy. The pathways of self-recovery were myriad, a labyrinth of

tunnels and dark corridors down which the individual and
the species had wandered to its position outside nature. The
answer lay in reversing the progress, in moving backward
toward a point of harmony in the collective past, where
youth, energy, and a binding relation to habitat could be
recaptured. In effect, Eshleman was working through
unbirths, sloughings of encrusted selves, to reacquire wholeness of imagination and feeling, though in the visionary
argument he develops the routes of his psychological
odysseys are always conceived as "re"-births.

> I love the incredible journey
> for its own screwdrivers
> & vises hung like beartraps
> on the inside of the image,
> for what happened IS the matter
> of the present compost—the lie
> of synapse is to make me think
> the terror could be shorter,
> but the coils of time digest me
> at their benign leisure . . .

(C 134)

Or this "birth/unbirth" from "The Ronin Cock" (*TGW* 106),

> . . . In 1947 I found myself
> a crawling spectre, I do not know how I got
> into that tight stuffed place, unceasing matter, it
>   was there
> my birth seemed to occur, I was utterly amazed
> to find no birthright, no past, as I gnawed and tunneled
> I became conscious of a greater birth which sought
> to tell its story: it was 1953, I was still
> in matter yet my body sat without, on a tower,
> a lifeguard, a private pool, daily I would gaze
> across the swimmers to the sun deck. Why pulled
> there I would ask myself, until I realized my attention
> was really under the deck, that's right, a one foot

area just big enough to crawl in, I wanted to
put lovers there, build a box for them to struggle
in, and I saw then I sought love but because
I had never experienced another I kept that crawl
area intact, a box, a place of self-struggle. I saw
myself walk the pool, life guard, I realized I stood
in a future reincarnation, I saw the karmic implications of
the whole cock, I saw my fate was to guard that life
which breaks free, which enters the world without
background, my fate was to feel stuck
with my own birth, be jealous of my
lost but vital crawling—if I accepted my fate
I would see this crawling life as the only
life and become its guardian, it would become
my lifework and thus I would never find
a real other, a person, to replace this crawling
lost one.

"The incredible journey" is a rescue expedition through a contemporary industrial setting, the mock-wilderness of America where the bear-traps are now implements of the mechanical age. The landscape itself is memory, the past, the "coils of time" which he moves through in reverse, being digested as he gropes backward to his origins. As with the other arts of the century, poetry's plot became retrogressive, a surge back into time away from the entropic end-zone of the "present compost." The image of a journey through tunnels of time forecasts Eshleman's later poetry on the Dordogne caves, whose limestone corridors are the litho-uterine passages in which he dramatizes a return to ultimate human origins and his own re-birth. But the image of time as a gut in which thought or identity is digested leads us back to the "lower body" as a landscape of mind—womb, gut, seat of the soul, or center of primordial consciousness. In Olson's essay, "Proprioception," the gut meets an unmediated earth through its ingestion of food. Eshleman's point in this passage from *Coils* is to suggest that the motion backward of recollection brings one down into the body, one's own, then the womb, and finally, the earth itself, the underworld. The flow of cultural energies has led to mind; the reversed odyssey brings one into the dark of unconsciousness, the flesh. Shimmering in the backdrop of this and similar passages is the thick foliage of the primal world, the rain forests accessible only by rivers, paths, whose windings into the "interior" struck Conrad's narrator Marlow as a kind of dissolution or devouring of self by nature, a devouring Erich Neumann would have equated with the recapture of the ego by the devouring womb of the Great Mother. Casting for an image of the poem as it first formed in the unconscious, Eliot called this stage of writing the "dark embryo," as if to say that a part of the mind was a womb.

By mid-century Western narrative had come to a grinding halt and began flowing backward. Narrative "progress" had been slowing all through the century, as narrators shot glances over their shoulders at the retreating past, and began finding themselves increasingly drawn to a past through flashbacks and reveries, elaborate reconstructions of history within the suspended present, as in Faulkner's *As I Lay Dying*. Indeed, suspension of the present for relentless analysis, in the *nouveau roman* and in John Barth's "literature of exhaustion," marked the point at which narrative stalled, and meandering recollection took over, a language laden with the imagery of the emotional past. Proust and Joyce explored the reversal of narrative early in the century, which Faulkner appropriated to treat the South. Eliot's *Four Quartets* is among the first poems of the post-war era to experiment with the "Moebius" strip of forward and reversed action:

> Time present and time past
> Are both perhaps present in time future
> And time future contained in time past.

But almost from the very start of modernism, lyric has meant a return to remote zones of the past. Western narrative had become a distillation of causality rooted in Western metaphysics, which mimicked and confirmed the seemingly inexhaustible goals of social advancement. Progress had no foreseeable end; the individual life cast upon the fictional landscape was propelled forward by the lure of goals and ambitions. The horizon forever receded with yet ungrasped mastery and rewards, which beckoned the protagonist to reach more deeply into his own potential to realize them. Conrad's Mr. Kurtz is among the first "flowers of Europe" to have been pitched headlong backwards into the primal abyss of human evolution, to emerge as more savage than the natives around him. His failure to attain the central goal of his company, the subjugation and exploitation of a backward people, is the "horror" which must be concealed by Marlow even from Kurtz's "Intended," though not, of course, from the reader. By 1950, the future ceased to be the upward path of the Western pilgrim; it was blocked at one end by the menaces of the Atomic Age. The horizon now brimmed with images of holocaust and cosmic ruin. The solution to atomic warfare was to retreat from its technology, to retrace one's steps and settle upon an antecedent stage of self-protection, some lower level of warfare's technology. Progress had been thwarted, but already the Western narrative of causal progression had lost most of its momentum; the 1950s were an anticlimactic revelation of the end of progress itself. This dilemma at midcentury produced an "apocalyptic fervor," Eshleman wrote recently, "a desperate effort to overwhelm what had been building in people since Auschwitz and Hiroshima: that the tumblers had been set not for an Edenic return, or advance into Aquarius, but for world destruction. For if there is no future and therefore no serviceable past, the present might resemble a flux of instantaneously equal alternatives, slipping forward from second to second, with each second, or sentence, supplanting the last" (*AS* 245–53). This was "atomic consciousness," according to Eshleman, with its "abstract interiors" in John Ashbery's hallucinatory lyrics, and the "wrecked phrases of Charles Bernstein (poems which resemble an endless string of rear-ended Laurel and Hardy autos)." Indeed,

> Bernstein and other "Language Poets" represent a new strategy for resistance to the accommodation of the American present. The accommodation is in how his poetry imitates the frenzied particle flow of our times, restricting content to buds of noticings that flicker like a grid flashing lights or disappear like snowflakes. The resistance is in his refusal to allow himself to be read with the gamut of sentimental response that characterizes middle-class identification with art. His internalized, non-referential punning forces the reader into the jungle-gym of syntax, and insists upon reader-participation to the extent that it is the reader who must organize what is traditionally called "meaning" in the poem. The extent to which Bernstein's poetry is a perceptive "reading" of our age and to what extent it is Dadaesque contempt for outworn modes remains open to question.
>
> ("Stevens-Artaud Rainbow")

As narrative action decelerated in the early years of 20th century literature, the tendency was intersected by the development of motion pictures, which possessed the mechanical function of reversal; the forward progress of cinematic plot was immediately reversed at the flick of a projector switch, a surprise pattern which provoked laughter when it was introduced into film comedy. At first, it was only a novelty of a mechanical medium, and the sight of crowds or traffic rushing backward, or of the Keystone Kops swiftly reversing their steps, had a wildly humorous effect

149

upon an audience. These episodes of reversal cast a satirical mood over the whole of a comedic narrative, and sowed a seed of doubt in progress itself. It was a tactic to be used delicately, as no more than an insinuation, whose skeptical consequences rippled across the course of a film's story. Once a reversal occurred, it broke the spell of progression, exposing it as an illusion imposed upon events. A comic figure who reversed his steps raised a profound laughter at his grim determination; within the ironic boundaries of mechanically controlled progression, life was reversible without consequence. The figure on the screen moved forward and backward with the same seriousness of purpose, as the philosophical debasement of progress insinuated itself. In these farcical interludes, 19th century fiction itself was raised to satirical inspection, and greeted with a boisterous guffaw in the 20th century.

By the 1950s, plot motion moved casually forward and back, by splicing and jump-cutting, cinematic devices imported into fiction and poetry; by juxtaposition, a modernist convention; by dialogical interaction within the same voice, or by circuitous meditation within monologue. As Eshleman put it:

> I see no need to eliminate a narrative context in which a self (personal or transpersonal) is struggling with its fate. However, if such a self is conscious of the extent to which it is a fleck in the global network, "free" and "imprisoned" as an American citizen, and at the center of a panopticon that includes an ecological deathrow as well as a cosmic library, then poetry is seen both as a synthesis *and* a melee, and I do not mean this thematically: I mean a progress of writing that *involves a ceaseless shifting of gears, backwards and forwards, at the same time,* a kind of poetry that faces what America is doing right now to Nicaragua at the same

moment it does not sweep aside the pleasures of physical existence.

("Stevens-Artaud Rainbow")

Time was a heavily trafficked route maze, in which forward motion had lost much of its ideological value, and reverse motion possessed complex psychological meaning. The blocked "ending" and the passage upstream in time entered midcentury drama through theater of the absurd, notably in Beckett's plays *Waiting for Godot* (1953), *Endgame* (1957), *Happy Days* (1958), and perhaps especially *Krapp's Last Tape* (1963), with its motif of a "former self" reappearing through the birthday tapes of earlier years. Sam Shepard's *The Unseeen Hand,* produced in 1969, uses retrogression in the postmodern sense in a scene in which a character begins repeating backwards the clichés and inanities another character has recited with devotion. Only then does the unseen hand of repression lift from his head and transfer its imprint onto the other character, a "cheerleader" for the doings of the small American town of Azusa. The retrogressive monologues of psychotherapy set the direction of writing in the post-war era—thinking backwards to traumatic youth and even beyond was the goal of post-war therapy and literature.

> Poetry had begun to mean something, I was out
> of verse up against my life Against biological
> energy that if not allowed out interferes
> with thought. This was the experience of my life
> to this point, to know that the world is Mental
> there is no such thing as *objective reality*
> The world we are begins in our biology
> before we are born, but that birth is
> as nothing Poetry is all about being reborn.

(*C* 50)

III

In 1984, Eshleman compiled an edition of selected work from the more than fifty books and pamphlets of his writing career. It was a formidable task indeed; not only did the selected edition limit him to only two hundred fifty pages of text, the circuitous routes of his poetry had now to be squeezed into a single narrative. Eshleman toyed with several notions of a possible "plot" for his book, and sought the advice of other writers and friends on the "best" of his work. After many revisions and ruminations, the book that emerged, *The Name Encanyoned River* (1986), condensed his canon to the bare essentials of his autobiography, trimmed and structured in such a way as to heighten by simplifying their dramatic breakthroughs and reversals. Reading *The Name Encanyoned River* by itself, without the benefit of the vast work behind it, gives one the impression of a life far more purposeful and pursued than the one elaborated in all this published material.

The collection opens with "Evocation I" from *Mexico & North,* and shows the first-time reader a voice just forming from its ventures into unfamiliar terrain: "Ajijic / beggars," a "python of backs / snailing /   / to the muddy chancel / where St. Anthony is crowned." St. Anthony, whose visions in the desert emptied out the sordid monsters of his unconscious, subtly reminds us of the process only just beginning with the young poet's forays into elemental Mexico. The "crowning" of St. Anthony is a fluid image, pointing ambiguously to a halo and to a culmination of events portraying St. Anthony's double nature as saint and bedevilled mortal. But the poem is, after all, only an "evocation," a tangential confrontation with these difficult issues; it only hints at the struggles that lay ahead of a poet wishing to reach the bottom of his own psyche. The opening poem of "The Coastal Ovens," section one of the book, summons a multitude of traditions behind postmodern poetry. Not only does Flaubert's *Temptation of St. Anthony* (1874) have its influence, but the forces of late 19th century Europe leading to post-Impressionism and Modernist poetics are called up by a few allusive details. More germane to the approach of "The Coastal Ovens" is its *ab initio* biography, reminiscent of Joyce's opening in *Portrait of the Artist as a Young Man* (1916). Eshleman's is a delayed awakening by the raw sensuality of Mexican life. All the palliatives of Indiana are torn away to expose the dormant soul coming to, reviving at the odors of unmediated life. This premise is a formal axis to the whole canon, its most fundamental principle: that all the ills of mankind are the wages of repression, and that rejuvenation lay in pilgrimages to the remote anteriors of human life, the "odor of earth" and "menstrual linens" in the scene before him.

Eshleman follows "Evocation I" with the opening poem of *Indiana*, "The Crocus Bud," which reinforces the theme of awakening. And with these "prefaces" established, the anchoring poem of the section can now be introduced, a shorter version of "The Book of Yorunomado" written in 1964. "The Coastal Ovens" follows the plot of death and renewal in Olson's *In Cold Hell, In Thicket* (1953), Levertov's *With Eyes at the Back of Our Heads* (1959), and Duncan's *The Opening of the Field* (1960), chronicles of poets who win back their natural sympathies in the industrial waste-land. Eshleman's sparer version of this plot describes him as pinned beneath a weight of prescriptions and falsifications of experience which he pries off at last. Though *Indiana* tells the story with more subtlety and psychological detail, the argument is carried more boldly in the few poems he chose for *Name Encanyoned River*. His maturer vision wrings from the original poems something new, a firmer gathering of loose ends, particularly in the close, where he atones for his excesses as rebel and reformer. With a turn of surrealist wit, he imagines himself rejoining the family whose bloodlines were a dead end for him not long before. The older poet regrets some of the slashwork and bitterness that came with his ambition to become an artist. Now his whole genealogy assembles before him in "The Bridge Over the Mayan Pass" to receive a mixture of apologies, blessings, reconciliations, though even here, bile mixes easily with balm. The Eshlemans gather "over the abyss" on a precarious rope bridge, including son Matthew, ex-wife Barbara, his remote ancestry, as Eshleman cries out

NOW TAKE OFF INDIANA
I RELEASE INDIANA

These demands are no sooner uttered than a distorted echo of them returns:

NAILED MILE GALED IN ANSWER
TRACED IN HEIL THY NATURN FACE!

They elude sense as a crumpled version of the first plea; directed at the father, Ira, who is the subject of this elegy, the language fuses wrangling images into a sing-song rhyme. "Nailed," "galed," "traced" and "face" force emphasis on the long "a" and "mile," "heil," "thy" alternate with the long "i". The "nailed" points toward Christ, one image of the male paternity, the "heil" to Hitler, the dark father; they balance the portrait of the male line from crucified son to crucifying father, both contained in the "naturn face," which hangs in the mist of the Mayan Pass, a dissolved but pervasive presence of the father. Indeed, such garbled speech expresses the anguished relation of the son; his mashed syllables, compressed to the point of incoherence in "nailed mile galed," though in "naturn" are resonances with "saturn," the long face of the father, possibly even "pattern," etc. Distorted speech appears crucially in another poem about his parents, "Deeds Done and Suffered by

Light" (*NER* 230–32), a sardonic elegy in dialogue between the son and his dead and buried parents. At one point, the father asks what Gladys needs from the supermarket, *"Gladys what do you want?"* but Gladys continues her rambling monolog from below, reminiscent of Beckett's chattering Winnie in *Happy Days,* until the father bellows his garbled demand, "GRADDISTROTDRURUNT." The mother is unavailing, but the distortion has worn down the literal phrase and exposed its ambiguity as an ultimate question, posed by father and son.

"The Coastal Ovens" closes with the son before his buried tormentors in "The Bridge at the Mayan Pass," but this truncated plot is the product of selecting and juxtaposing poems out of a larger context. The poems cover the decade of the 1960s and show a son squabbling with elders, toiling after his freedom, becoming a young father himself, last seen in a rage talking back to the ghost of his father. But individual poems undermine the plot, and when heeded closely, create an ambiguous second theme running counter to the main theme of the text. Several of the poems take their start in the speaker's anger or frustration, leading him backward not just to youth, but to the primordial source of being, the womb. A poem begins in pangs of remorse and sends him back to the mother he had tried so vigorously to elude. The psyche of the poet drops deeper into the abyss with each presumed step forward toward maturity. "Evocation I" opens the book with a glimpse at a balustrade where "broken steps" spill an "alphabet of stone." These elements are reconstituted in "The Bridge at the Mayan Pass" in much altered form: the balustrade is now a "rope bridge," and the broken steps descend into an abyss of the earth, a vaginal fissure over which Eshleman's lineage perilously congregates for a picnic. "Lean into wind," the speaker tells himself in "Evocation I," but now he *is* the wind, a cry for freedom from his profound oppression in "The Bridge." The scene of his musings is the primal landscape of Mexico, the "dawn" of experience, the deepest past where "a new day" is balanced between "a child" and "a fresh kill," both enclosed by the "rain of blackberries / on rusted / / stone." The modern self enters a landscape of origins where nothing has fallen into separate existence. The "I" is the sorrows of modernity, the "weighted dread" at the end of many civilizations. The primordial landscape is so jumbled and freakish his own infantile beginnings are aroused as he lowers *into* its primal embrace. His rage and resentment in "The Bridge" are directed at his isolation from experience, the cold, hard shape of his identity. For this, he blames the father, indeed all fathers of historic patriarchy:

> I HATE STONE, I bring pieces of it into my room only
>   to weight the pages from the wind
> on which the honest words of men who have lived
>   through their lives live!
> I HATE THE STONE IN MAN
>
> . . . I hate you because you are simply a cruddy
>   uninteresting piece of this history!

Finally,

> THE MEANING OF STONE IS
> IT BE FUCKED ON OVER A BED OF
> DOWN EVERY SECOND DAY IN THE LIFE OF MAN

>   (*NER* 66)

These lines run together Olson's precept in "The Kingfishers" to "hunt among stones" with an episode in his "Song of Ullikumi" where the female powers of the earth, the "mountain," are repeatedly "fucked" by the fledgling god Kumarbi, to gain his manhood. Eshleman later worked out his own rendering of the song in "A Note and a Fantasia on Ullikummi" (included in *Hotel Cro-Magnon*), to

156

describe such intercourse with the "huge rock" as a breaking down of "earth's resistance." The child of this relation is Ullikummi, who is cut away from earth to begin the age of "patriarchal seeding," thus ending "matriarchal parthenogenesis." In the early poem, the "stone in man" is the resistant, inert substance of masculine ego; later, Eshleman gradually reversed himself by calling Earth the stone on whom the male gods won their sovereignty; the same stone forms the walls of Lascaux in "Visions of the Fathers of Lascaux," where male priests drew a human effigy from its limestone "womb," and fashioned a patriarchal ruler over the female Earth. The word "stone" has two values in the poetry; it is the bleak mineral of masculinized will, the emblem of his father Ira; but stone is also the material of a female Earth, the rock-bodied Gaia, a pliant, fertile matter (*mater*) endlessly creating life from its labyrinthine interiors. *Hotel Cro-Magnon* opens on this theme of the creativity of earth and rock in the poem "Apotheosis," which describes the Brittany coast:

> Where clouds
> temple the horizon, realms of whitened
> rock enfold light,
> vast inorganic fruit. Grandeur:
>
>   unfurling arabesques
> that confirm parthenogenesis.
> The bay is swooned with streaks of cobalt, jade,
> "granit rose," pink and black speckled rock
>   dolmen-contoured in soft
> lifting heaps, or saucers. In this light,
> the pink and black meld to tawny rose, living rock,
>   *rose rock!*
> One need go no further for satisfaction with the earth.
>   "Nature is imagination itself"

The conventional male is thus stoney, but the stones are things within a living, procreative system. It is only by cutting oneself off (like Ullikummi or "Lascaux") from maternal energy that one becomes hardened, insensitive, unyielding. The melt-down of intellect by hallucinogenic drugs in the 1960s came to be known as "getting stoned," a phrase which obliquely concurs with Eshleman's feminine sense of the word. The stone chasm at the "Mayan Pass" points to a matriarchal past, the rock ledges of a dark, twisting vaginal abyss where the Eshleman line stands in ghostly reunion. The Eshlemans have come full-stop into the Ahabian age, and have left behind the last son, whose rage is directed against the dead end his family has brought him to; he imagines them on a bridge that leads backward in time toward the promise of an unspecified redemption, which lay somewhere in the rock recesses of the pre-Columbian past.

What She Means (1978) drops organized narrative and floats poems in a mosaic suspension. The title puts emphasis on the "she," an ambiguous referent pointing to a "red spider," to his wife Caryl, to females and mythological femininity, which occupies a considerable part of the poetry. The "she" is the lost dimension of masculine imagination, the "rock":

> that "she"
> must invade. Centuries of rock
> in man's will against
> her active participation
> in the crucial space between
> his life and her poem.

("Alleluia Choruses," *WSM* 73)

Eshleman's preoccupation with feminine nature links the poems to main issues of the decade: the feminist revolution and the determined effort by many forces to redefine

Western civilization in terms of sexual conflict and the history of female "colonializing." But there are long stretches of flaccid writing that leave the impression these arguments are nascent speculations lacking in vigor or vividness for the poet. Already one may discern a second argument beginning to emerge here and there in references to the Dordogne and to Paleolithic cave culture. *What She Means* marks a transition from personal to mythological identity, as Eshleman broadens the meaning of his emotional life to stand for events, rituals, crises defining generic human identity.

Hence the title *What She Means,* in which a redefining process takes up all the terms so far established in his autobiography. This accounts in part for the waffling language, where once crisply plotted events slowly lose their sharp edges and become partly fantasized or mythologized recollections. Nothing literal remains; the imagination has begun investing particulars with a certain generality and distortion. Eshleman seems no longer bent on absolving himself or of escaping from his childhood dilemmas but in "translating" a life as if it were an encoded text, a language of experience he had been only partially rendering into personal speech. His own life had become a Vallejo poem requiring a leap in thought and attitude to bring it fully to life on paper. The poems must now step back and reconsider the conceptual approach he had taken. The "she" is now to be regarded as both mother and nature, as biological parent and as the creative earth. Gladys is suddenly an array of potential deep images to be called forth by the mythical imagination. The question asked earlier, "Gladys what do you want?" seems hurled not so much at the dead mother as at the Earth. The question was posed by both father and son in that poem, and through the blurred edges of mythological imagination we sense the question is ultimately metaphysical: Why are we here? What is this life you created for us? Gladys is thus mother (Earth) and these are her bewildered children. Hence, the question of feminine identity underlying *What She Means*. The poet has discovered his own life is a series of obscure deep events, demanding a different imaginal engagement for their understanding.

The mythological process finally leads back to the poet's own perception of his adult self—as linked twins, a self and this "other" with whom he sometimes thinks and grasps the pattern of his life. The interior life is thus an erratic dialog between a literalizing ego, the waking conscious voice of thought, and a primal other, the soul, the mythological self whose existence is part of the mind's underworld, the realm of image and spirit. It is only through this other self within that the depths of a life can be understood and seen from a long perspective—the living conscious self as an atom within a vast historical process. The mythological imagination grasps origins and sources, and makes stories of existence based on *ex nihilo* beginnings.

Eshleman's preoccupation with his own youth suddenly widens into a mythic quest for the youth of the species in the womb passing all through the limestone caves of the Dordogne. The house at 4705 Boulevard Place, Indianapolis, built of red brick and timbers, is a ghostly descendant of the caverns of the Vézère River in Southwestern France where Gladys obliquely reappears as the Venus of Lespugue and his father as a stooped, stone-chipping hunter-gatherer, a fatal interruptor of primordial bliss the moment he sets hand to pigment and begins defining the limits of human identity on the walls of his cave. Origins no longer stop at the crib and the baby book, or the slaughterhouse; they reach back into the female earth to the first scratchings of imagination on bones and rocks.

Eshleman's preface associates the meandering nature of his new poetry with the "core meanders" of an incised ox-rib from hominid prehistory, 300,000 B.C.; both represent efforts to create history, "to find out," i.e., an out, "or exit, for the self." His "meanders" are a means of extending his narrative beyond self; he dismisses the notion of "free association" or of "automatic writing" in his poetry, even though his "thought" is open to "twist, dissolve, whatever, out of my own experience." Indeed, "background and childhood [will] continue," but "as agents of composition, taking on different meanings, as opposed to disappearings, as I age." By such means, "the 'other' comes in, not only as that numinous presence about me in which I sense Caryl's multifoliate meaning, but other people, out there, in America and beyond."

His forays into his own past, the garden of fading memories and subliminal crises, are, to use Jung's term, the "enantiodromic" subplot, the forward and backward flow of thinking, of *What She Means*. In such struggles against time, an "opposite" self forms as his hated double, the rejected potentials of the actual self. Indeed, the mature soul is forlorn over the loss of its unlived twin; much of Eshleman's metaphoric language transposes things across one self to its buried other, smuggling the present into the trapped past. The chimerical figures of his best poetry steal things from waking reality to furnish a disappearing world. Such poetic maneuvers set Proust on his head, as Eshleman tries to feed *memory* with what is here and now. The sensual recreation of a contemporary scene is fed into the emotional past, where "a child / calls back to us / with everything we can possibly imagine we are" (*A* 101).

The emergence of the double self in these poems is a complicated and only partly developed theme. By childhood we must suppose Eshleman means the adolescent self in which infancy is gone and an ego is pretty well shaped in him. By adolescence the crises of youth have hardened into a fixed formula of emotions and attitudes, the very figure who heads for Mexico in the summer of 1957; but now there is this more supple and emotionally liberated adult who no longer yearns to repossess *this* aspect of his youth. In fact, his enriched maturity, his feminized persona, can now look back with considerable scorn at the raw materials his adolescence represents. And the more youthful double comes in for a scolding by the wiser, and in some ways much younger adult spirit. The quarrels that ensue in the poems make an odd sort of closet theater of the bickering voices of modern consciousness. One voice is the postmodernized persona, resensitized and able to juggle his contrarieties with quiet assurance; the figure he addresses in his own mind is the rough, pubescent male whom society indifferently slung together in its instutitions. The internal dialogs Eshleman constructs are between two rival versions of selfhood: the one fashioned by an errant culture and the other reconceived by means of an adversarial esthetic tradition. The one self peers down at the creature whom he dismantled and put back together; they face off against one another at last.

> What is virgin or just beginning to be experienced
> is destroyed before it is fully there.
> In ceremonies that pretended to carry us across
> from being boys to being men the actual transition
> was from a pledge trembling in bunny-footed p.j.s at
>   a midnight "line-up"
> to an active with a paddle pinned to a girl from a
>   good sorority,
> TV holding hands Saturday evening or when the
>   weather was good
> the fratfire at Dunn's farm with songs,
> that maniacal presence where the pines began
> as if our relative, Manson, wanted to join us, all
>   bloody wanting
> to be part of our evening.

> ("Still-Life, with Fraternity," *WSM* 63)

We find the newly confident adult even going back to his old mentor, Vallejo, in "The Name Encanyoned River," to bid him farewell. He is through being his apprentice, Eshleman tells him, now that he has achieved his own maturity by successfully rendering Vallejo's poems in *The Complete Posthumous Poetry*. Now this other ghost of his imagination, his haunting double, must also be sent back to the void, though this youth, the *puer*, cannot be expelled so easily. Eshleman grapples with a new subtlety of mind: how youth shrinks into a fossilized second self who reappears as an echoey antagonist in one's middle age. Maturity has a way of clearing out the background of memory, and as these longings for a lost innocence evaporate, a pale ghost of the old self lingers on whom he disagrees with as if he were chastising his own son. This figure of himself in miniature takes the place of Matthew as Eshleman summons the wisdom his father never gave him. Eshleman is now his own father, the one he wanted and whose functions he now provides. In effect, these poems shift the locus of imagination from the remaking of the son to the remaking of the father, so that the two voices are a projected father to an imaginary son, both figments of the persona's memories and emotions. In "Still-Life, with Manson," Eshleman no longer yearns to relive his past, instead he gives himself a good lecturing on the meanness of his youth. There are now in him "the ghosts of / the fathering mothering powers I / can transform to aid me," he tells himself in "The Dragon Rat Tail." "At 40," it's time to drive away this shrunken, malformed other of his thoughts:

> Confidence
> I pray, at 40, to lead this doppelganger out to pasture,
> he cannot be done with
> I can only let him graze,
> I am his shepherd, linked to

him Americanwise through Harlem,
through Chile, through Iran.

(WSM 56)

This ghostly *puer* has become a sort of gargoyle of misshapen sexual desire, and Eshleman now reinterprets those rituals of his fraternity days as grotesque theater, where the sensitivity he might have developed was pulled out of him. In "Still-Life, with Manson," Eshleman extends his thesis that males are deformed at puberty to include this study of Manson's childhood, which he describes in terms of an Aztec sacrifice where the heart is torn out and fed to the sun, another patriarchal symbol:

> That hard thigh coated with hose
> was the screen onto which I
> and my Indianapolis friends were projected, ant
> ticks in the pompom machine, our destruction
> intimate with our growth. We were joined
> by the death of whatever surge there was in puberty,
> Charlie Manson, an altar,
> over which, spread-eagled, his heart was
> torn from his chest and held to the sun,
> and the sun, extending what I can only describe as
>   a goiter-filled
> viper-coiled claw, took his little boy heart, tasted it,
>   grimaced,
> and spat the tasted bit back into his face.
> For us, survival was assured.

(61)

The long years of reconstructive adult thought have laid bare the brutal conventions of male-rearing, which Eshleman scrutinizes in his poetry. One virtue of adulthood is the understanding of having been shattered at youth, and of having the power to reconvene all the parts. The polarization has consequences for both genders. Wakoski's poetry also launches an extended inquiry into her youth as a female growing up in the drab world of California farm laborers. In her book *Smudging,* the same process of gender polarity, hyperfeminization, isolates her from natural desire, the instinctual world she sees at a distance, through another window, flickering in a forbidden world. She associates youth, in the title poem of the book, with hours spent in dread and fascination of a world of tequila-drinking men, who return in her poetry in the guise of lovers of all sorts, and of the missing father whom she fantasizes into a host of companions, demons, kings, spirits, and her own sheared-away masculine dimension. "Smudging" captures the longings of female childhood in much the same terms Eshleman depicted his male growing up, as we see her dawdling away an evening trying to imagine the life of pickers huddled over the smudge pots used in the citrus groves, a world kept out of her reach throughout her pubescent years. Her recovery takes nearly the same course as Eshleman's: a retracing of the steps of growing up to the point at which traumatic rearing pulled her apart and forced her into passive femininity.

Eshleman's subsequent poetry involves the function of the orgasm as a way of breaking down differences between the sexes, of merging and enriching self through loving contact with the other. The sexual act is sacramental in the poems, a mythical reenactment of a return to the womb and underworld by the male, and a repossession of lost male powers by the female. Orgasm is the ecstatic reunification of a "whole" self, a resolution of anguished sexual polarity. Eshleman's prefaces increasingly assert the collaborative role of his wife Caryl in the act of writing, editing, arranging the poems of his books, thus extending the sexual union to matters of art, work, daily life in a reconstructed, equalized, marriage. The domestic reforms heralded in the poems of *What She Means* substitute for the social activism of other poets; if Eshleman can set his own house in order, and restore the sexual and mental compatibility between sexes under his own roof, he achieves in microcosm the rebuilding of a world at large. The political message of the poems is usually disseminated through personal experience, but occasionally erupts into declamatory outbursts on the feuding (and feudal) temperament of the West toward Third World countries.

Whereas Rothenberg and Wakoski frequently explore their racial and sexual persecution, Eshleman makes atonement as a member of the persecuting majority. His redemption comes by joining the other side, by a fusion of self with the otherness long stifled by Western ideals. In his domestic revolution Eshleman freed himself from patriarchy by boldly revising his domestic and marital views, efforts which anticipated not only feminist assaults on patriarchal authority, but the widespread effort to reform civil rights in the post-imperial age. Eshleman's wife embodies not only his opposite sexual nature, she borders on a world of intuitive lore and sympathy extending from the deepest past to those ex-colonies running along the perimeters of industrial civilization. Apotheosizing Caryl and sharing the work with her as equal partner is akin to the massive energies Eshleman has poured into his translations of the rebel voices of Peru, Chile, the Caribbean, and Europe. A baptism into a world of otherness has been the absorbing drama of Eshleman's career as a writer.

In his "Preface" to *What She Means,* Eshleman notes that "the attempt to get rid of the 'I' is as crippling as the attempt to get rid of the 'other.' Both are valid points," like the "inner gold" and "surface iron" of another context. Conventions and patterns of verse must give in, must "warp" in the converging of both sides of human personality. This is the "voice coil" of the opening untitled poem, the slight warping of speech when the self's two voices talk at once; the result is a punning, allusive dialectic, as each side tugs discourse to its own realm:

                    Narcissus

              loosed

                 with an urn

          [becomes restated as]

              grip

                 of the iron

          [and then]

              grp of

                 the pond strangling i—

Narcissus, or ego, dragged down into the pond below its
reflection, into an underworld, loses the "i" in grip; "the
centering spider" tugs the ego into the depths of the unconscious and thus "aligns the voice coil of the magnetic /   /
gap" (*WSM* 13). The gap is that channel where discourse
runs, the magnetized banks of which are the two sources
of identity: the dark world of nature and the bright, orderly cosmos of human thought. The process by which one
"aligns the voice coil" and allows language to warp between
poles of self is a kind of creolizing of English, Eshleman's
own version of a subdialect within American speech. Only
this dialect distorts grammar, syntax, spelling, punctuation,
typography according to the nature within, an inward native
world. The result is one of the unique characteristics of his
verse hereafter—the coining of hybrid imagery and "corruptions" of orthodox usage as discourse runs a gauntlet of oppositions in the "magnetic gap." The hybrid images thrown
up by the process represent tiny but essential fusions

between rational and primitive faculties. Ginsberg's *Howl* employed the process first in celebrated conjunctions like "hydrogen jukebox," but Eshleman's hybrids go a step further by fusing terms to represent self in the grip of primal nature. In "The Name Encanyoned River," he thanks his mentor Vallejo for naming the channel in which true intercourse must flow—

> a river frozen between ego and other
> my senses could not thaw
> until I wept into you, got my tears in hand
> a cry for the infant of occasion to break
> through the back turned linoleum of the hardened
>   present
> world

> (*NER* 136)

Eshleman's main theme, in this and later books, is that modern life is increasingly abstract, in dread of its past and the influence of nature. The animal roots of human identity are forever being sheared away in abhorrence of a dark, mythical origin. In "The Cogollo," he puts the matter in the form of a sacrifice:

> Men live at a never ending sexual funeral
> where their ripped away Siamese twin is the stuff
>   in the casket,
> when they look closely he is the remains of a paleolithic
> bison, their real double, their 50% other, the animal
> they lost in their cavity, when eons ago they descended
> the pyramid's inner stairway to become ha ha immortal.

> (*NER* 69)

Everything humanity invents possesses a hybrid identity in which a modern form encloses ancient energies, as in "For Milena Vodickova," where Eshleman analyzes a familiar cartoon figure:

> I punctured a hole
> in Donald Duck, Pollock's
> "The Deep" showed
> the cenote
> under Duckberg
> Donald and his nephews were
> diving for Mayan treasure . . .

(NER 147)

In "Still-Life, with African Violets," the phrase "African Violets" slurs into "African violence," the "root" text that suddenly springs to the surface in this flower shop, one of many disguises to be rent and plundered for what lies beneath it as repressed (violent) reality:

> I will not try to balance myself on nothing,
> I will believe the enraged African is thicker
> than the Beverly Hills lady clerk, in doing so I will
>   betray
> my life a block south of Beverly Hills,
> my physical body is here with the retail violet
>   instead of with
> the violet of the earth; . . . .

(NER 133)

The notorious artificiality of life and art in Hollywood, near where Eshleman was living at the time, proffered a rich harvest for his satiric mill, but in general he has been sparing in his assaults on pop culture. His humor is not topical but Bakhtinian and derisive, feeding on selective, philosophically rich subjects that he can work into his general thesis that American life is a sexual wasteland without underworlds or mystery. Guided in general, I think by Norman O. Brown's vista on modern life as an illusory reality where death is made the enemy of individualism, Eshleman's primary targets are those social stereotypes in comic strips and cartoon animations where we see a radically simplified view of the individual or of nature—as with Dagwood and Blondie, or Uncle Scrooge and Donald Duck, and the real-life caricatures of the masculine in Hitler, Idi Amin, Charles Manson. Like Rothenberg, Eshleman is fascinated with Hitler especially, the ultimate masculine grotesque, whom both poets have satirically portrayed as having "tits," the symbol of the female so obviously missing from any of these figures of patriarchy and power. The key to Eshleman's mocking humor is its satire of male apotheosis in America, which he ridicules through the grotesque imagery of the unconscious, the very faculty excluded from the male's rational world.

One of his more daring assaults on an arch symbol of the male occurs in the poem "Joseph," where he makes some shrewd speculations about the nature of Joseph, the foster father, and Christ, the divine man as son. Here is the patrilineal line with a rich context of qualifying conditions lying at the heart of Christian partiarchal worship. In both roles Eshleman discerns certain denials of natural fatherhood and of filial relation: a father who has not conceived and a son who is not mortal. Eshleman supposes that here is the first clue of Christian squeamishness with sexuality, the root of its denials of the body and of the old Dionysian ecstasies of the flesh. The holy family is abstractly constituted with surrogates for the roles of actual father and son. Interrupting this analysis of Christ is a "long drip out of a dream," a voice from the depths of his "other" self, which asks the question, "Why have you not returned Hitler's tits." Even Eshleman takes pause over the evident nonsense of this question, which struck him as "so / irrational it seems as if I were joking." Immediately, however, Eshleman sets out to decode the riddle. Here is the maniacal, hypertrophic "father," the Fuehrer of Germany, a monstrous expression of masculine authority, the opposite of timid, almost sexless Joseph, the foster father. Hitler's devouring of the

Jewish population of Europe is the radical extreme of how
Joseph raises Christ, the Jewish son. Not only is Hitler the
negation of Joseph, he is himself negated by the "tits" ex-
pected of him in the odd phrase "from a dream." The unconscious "completed" Hitler in a way that might redeem
him, or at least abate his monstrosity: the question put to
Eshleman's rational side asks him to "return" the organ
necessary to balance the monstrous disproportion of a tyrant.
Hitler as archetypal father can be remade by returning the
suppressed, denied, half of his spirit: his femininity. Hitler's
monstrosity is his stoney masculinity; he is the soul of aggression and menacing hatred of any form of otherness to
the Aryan ideal. The voice "from a dream" speaks for nature
when it poses its question.

The last thirty pages of *What She Means* makes an exuberant demonstration of the potentials of hybrid language.
"As I get older," he writes, "the sides of life become denser
dreams" (158). The unified sensibility pitches everything into
its vibratory imagination, as he tests the limits of his new
style, the binary mode which he applies to a host of familiar
themes. "All books are 'dirty'"—begins "The Rancid
Moonlight Hotel," a poem combining spliced memory bits
and satiric commentary on the fake mysticism of Carlos
Casteñeda—because "they are built out of stimulated
organs." With this gambit, Eshleman stretches himself to
outrageous formulations, many of them brilliantly new, supporting a central trope, the "alligator, / witho't diaper,
dressed in his brain," the writer of so-called "dirty" books
whose double nature combines reptile and human
awareness.

The second section of poems in *The Name Encanyoned
River,* "Scorpion Hopscotch," is dominated by poems
selected from *What She Means.* Only one poem comes from
Coils, and a few others from *The Gull Wall.* Eshleman concentrates on poems that explore his relationships to other

people. "The Physical Traveler," from *Coils,* takes off on
Blake's "The Mental Traveler," and makes an allegory of
the soul as a "womblike form." The father, Ira, appears as
a rapist who has impregnated the son, who then "strove out
of Paradise" heavy with his own imminent rebirth. The
scene of the father's seduction is superbly condensed at the
close of the poem:

> for I remember my father
> I remember the night
> he crept into my cell
> & my crib ran red.

> (*NER* 73)

"I found a woman in my way," he says earlier, with the suggestion that she is Gladys, the mother; confronting her closes
the plot of "The Coastal Ovens" section, but rather than
destroy her or drive her from consciousness, he absorbs her
back into his psyche:

> I found a woman in my way
> She sat crouched in my passage
> head tucked between her
> knees, I tried to push her out

> I tried to see her face
> I couldn't budge her from the shaft
> & so I joined her to
> my fate by pushing her up

> Inside me through my recent
> gate.

> (*NER* 72)

"In Creation," he says, "each thing weds & / couterweds."
Parents are incorporated into the psyche as necessary opposition, a nourishing antithesis of his character. Hence, the

172

closing image of the father as succubus, whose seed is added to him in the crib, and who now labors with the figurative pregnancy of a new self. The following poem, "Study for a Self-Portrait at 12 Years Old," from *The Gull Wall,* extends the allegory from parents to grandparents, the second step of a journey through his genetic corridors, back to ultimate origins. In this poem, the son steals from his cot, leaving behind his Charlie McCarthy self as his double, to crawl beneath the sleeping parents' bed (which *had been* the grandparents' bed) "to join them," because "he had to go on":

> He bit
> into the tufted cover, gnawed a hole
> big enough to draw his head and shoulders
> into, losing all *sense* of them now,
> for once into it they seemed the other
> side of the world!
>
> (*NER* 75)

The other side of *time,* for his "gnaw and tunnel / gnaw and tunnel" is through and beyond them, devouring the life passage as he crawls through it: "body sludge or / bits of skin, . . . was it / theirs?" It *was* the flesh of his ancestry, parents "or people / like he'd seen in pictures of caves," but "impossible to know," which, as he "kept / pulling along with his loom-motion, new born but mountainously lost," becomes the image of birth *and* death:

> in what, when thought, appeared conception
> but, in movement, was burial, within which
> he was to go on and on.

It is burial to literally dig through the graves of one's lineage, and birth to pass up through the line of one's descent, continuously growing younger as one gnaws through the tunnel back to the "people / like he'd seen in caves." Subsequent poems of "Scorpion Hopscotch" elaborate the allegory of a man digging through time toward the intitial point of human energence. In "Creation," the "Venus of Lespugue" is introduced, a female statuette carved from a mammoth tusk in the Solutrean period (ca. 18,000 B.C.), and found in the Haute-Garonne region of France, whose ancestral link stretches his lineage across eons. Her enormous rump and breasts are celebrations of the Mother, "buried in gross / maternal body," and "in the place of parental stone" where

> I gnaw and tunnel
> feeling your living pressure in
> their bodies' dents
> I raise
> through you into
> that Venus,
> leaving my buttocks
> as a fly's eyes

(NER 77)

Now the "earth" itself is "foetal," an emblem of birth whose own evolutionary history is a maze of corridors and caverns leading backward to first things.

"Scorpion Hopscotch" compresses a prolific output of poetry from 1975 to 1979 into a few short poems that connect his early autobiographical poetry to the bolder allegories of *What She Means*. The figure who struggled to birth himself anew reappears as a mole gnawing through the ancestral labyrinth into the paleolithic era, to the birth of consciousness, behind which lay a shimmering terrain prior to thought. This is the "hopscotch" he plays through the squares of his ancestral descent; the game is played on a grid of interlocking genetic episodes, which are all prefigured in the orgasm, "a crystal ball" whose "marvelous inner workings" encode the destiny of the species. The outer boundary of this sphere is death, which forms the dialectic of life's great urge.

The profusion of themes and narratives which carry over from *What She Means* into "Scorpion Hopscotch" are Eshleman's response to middle age.

> One ages, and the meanings in amber and white
> repeat, nourish, even though one is reined to
> that Crusoe ghost, one's mind, that
> light, stucco, mist ignore
>
> ("A Late Evening in July," *WSM* 179)

"August, Senex," reminiscent of Olson's "The Distances," explores the male midlife defined by Jung and later by James Hillman in *The Puer Papers,* in which male sexual desire departs from the force of the ego and returns to consciousness as Cupid, Amor, or Eros, the ghosts of youth. Eshleman's version offers new embellishments:

> The puer had begun to grow little horns
> his body fuzzy, less substantial than when he spoke,
> but I recognized now a kind of impatience about him,
> had I put him in trousers too early?
>
> (*WSM* 99)

"A Climacteric" sorts out his perceptions on aging from a new perspective on the mother-son relation:

> I realized I will no longer
> dream of her turning aside
> and beckoning me to their bedside.

Though gone from mind, the mother will return linked to the memory of his father, and to other archetypal figures who make up the interiors of the poet at midlife. "Today," he notes, "I walked into my tomb," youth's sepulcher, in which his mother resides in "her surrounding nourishment." Things once driven out of mind drift back gracefully to recesses of thought, where they take up supportive roles in his awareness. The poet welcomes the return of once painful memories which he spins into lyrical elegies for youth. He is beyond the point of further change, and must accept the person he now is: a son *and* a father.

Chapter Four

"The Descent Beckons"

Without imaginal understanding, we may expect killing, as if our culture cannot ever take down the wild Western ego until it has restored the ancient sense of image and recovered the imaginal from the broken shards of reformational literalism.

James Hillman, The Dream and the Underworld
(115)

Pound opened the (revised) *Cantos* by translating Andreas Divus's Latin version of the *Odyssey*, Book XI, the journey to the land of the dead. It was 1923, a year after Joyce's *Ulysses* appeared from Shakespeare & Co., but Pound and Eliot had already expressed its influence in their work. Joyce's "Circe" chapter, later adapted for the stage as *Ulysses in Nighttown,* makes extensive use of Book XI of the *Odyssey,* with the dead appearing to both Bloom and Dedalus as each relived his traumatic past and came to terms in a friendship. Joyce overlaid his Odyssean myth with Dante's vision of purgatory, and the two major texts on the underworld became central to Modernist writing. Eliot's *The Waste*

Land depicts the Dantean underworld set in post-WWI London's financial district, "the City," and elsewhere.

The modern fascination with underworlds has a long provenance reaching back into the last century; its beginnings might be located in Darwin and Wallace, whose researches took them to regions "down under," to Galapagos and the Malay Archipelago, where links to pre-human history were puzzled out. These were natural junkyards where all the blind ends of evolution could be dug up and studied like shards of pottery. It was a recess of time, a dimension reaching back beyond record, a time in which the West ran out and disappeared into nature. The earlier researches of James Hutton and Charles Lyell, in the so-called "golden age" of geology, 1790–1820, had already postulated an "underworld" of time, a dark abyss of natural mysteries to which only a fossil record and the tormented rocks made any allusion. The Romantic Age had already passed through its first cycle, with its own profound vision of a living universe whose myteries mocked the explanations of Western empiricism.

By a curious twist, a purely mechanistic explanation of nature did not emerge from the scientific opportunity to rewrite human genesis. A new mysticism crept into the narrative puzzle of natural history; the unwilled phenomema of nature possessed levels of inexplicable creativity and purposefulness which conferred upon its mute immensity a sort of brooding intelligence far grander than human intelligence. In postulating such a hypothesis about nature, it would seem that the sturdy philosophical materialism of modern Western thought had found its own flaw, through which a number of mystical insights made their way into 19th century discourse. The more firmly entrenched was the rationalist, mechanistic regime of the industrial age, the more the pure sciences and arts began shifting attention to natural history, the past, where certain anticipations of philosophical renewal began mounting. The past was the uncodified but largely abandoned evidence of nature's formative powers, of which the present was a curious disjunction, since it bore all the distinctions of having been humanly determined, an orchestration of events under the control of human will. Perhaps that is why, in 1912, the sinking of the Titanic seemed a momentously catastrophic event far in excess of its actual loss of life and treasure. The unsinkable ship was an emblem of human control which nature had easily, even casually, sent to the underworld.

No sooner had Darwin set out to contruct a narrative of the deep past, a modern Homer linking up episodes and anecdotes into a composite account of an epic hero, than others set out alongside him to pursue the past differently, as a haven from the sterility and entrapments of modern urban life. Gauguin began depicting the remote human past through his paintings and sketches of Tahitian tribal life— its sexual freedom, communal bonds, myths and beliefs. His bright primary colors were an affirmation of this island in time; he sketched the living past with the same enthusiasm Darwin filled his notebooks on fossil remains. But the thick columns of paint and broad beam-like forms that make up his characters were the fundamentals of a new perception. When Roger Fry described the work of Gauguin, Cézanne, Van Gogh and others as Post-Impressionism, he meant to distinguish their exploration of under-surfaces of things from the purely sensory world of Impressionist art. Under the appearances of conventional reality were geometrical forms— right angles, circles, squares, cylinders, triangles, the archetypes of identity lying just beneath the surface of mundane life. These were the "bones" of reality, the primordial patterns of daily experience. The Post-Impressionist painting made an x-ray of appearance and discovered the deep past residing in its structural interior. In poetry, the same conclusion is drawn through the use of historical personae: the mythological consciousness of Tiresias in *The Waste Land,* a witness across time and space to the eternal drama of sexual treachery and betrayal, to the death of the gods and the depravity of life without them. Pound's persona in *The Cantos* is not one consciousness but the collective consciousness of poets across the whole of Western civilization, the mind-stream running down through literary history. *Ulysses* is a sustained palimpsest in which the Homeric world shimmers translucently beneath the detailed chronicle of a day in modern Dublin. The mythic underworld lingering like a universalized residue in each scene of *Ulysses* occupies the same function as geometry in painting, and mythology and history in poetry. Reality was not merely the sum total of fleeting coincidence, the random events of an inert universe; appearance was a skin stretched tight over the underworld itself, in whose depths were the fundamentals of nature.

Getting to the bottom of reality was the absorbing preoccupation of Modernist art as well as the social sciences. In 1900, Freud's *The Interpretation of Dreams* showed that cognition itself was organized into a surface reality and a deep reservoir of natural and recurrent forms, of which the dream state was a base. Either all forms of human behavior converged to the sexual urge, as Freud believed, or the base was lower still, more remote, extending down into the undifferentiated awareness of primitive life forms, the involuntary functions of the "reptile brain." As Wyndham Lewis once declared, the true poet bore the memory of the fish. The human brain was its own Galapagos Island, a surface of fleeting events and impressions over the strata of experience that ranged down to the beginnings of life. These beginnings drifted up into thought in the geometrical simplicity of myths, hunches, intuitions, inspired ramblings, primitive rites, dreams, spells, fevers, states induced by drugs, alcohol, hypnotism. The unconscious was simultaneously the irrational and the human past, madness or darkness and the eons of experience prior to individuality or subjective isolation. The underworld itself was merely time, experience impacted behind a civilization experimenting with the limits of pure consciousness and the curious structures it built in thought: the self, logical systems, the sufficiency of civilization. As the surface of Western certainty grew thin, all life became the palimpsest in which to glimpse the underworld of time. The sciences probed time in the interest of settling the issue of ultimate origins; through the telescope space turned into time as one peered backward through the exploding universe to its closing nuclear genesis. Space probes in the postmodern era were also justified as necessary explorations of Earth's origins. The underworld was overhead, within, below, and behind the contemporary Westerner.

The financial collapses in Europe and the U.S. in the 1930s temporarily diverted artistic attention to contemporary problems, the decade in which Pound dwelt on modern political history and economic themes, as the rest of literature took up various positions on the wisdom of capitalism. Since the U.S. market crash had precipitated economic events in Europe, it was clear that Europe was now reacting to, not originating the circumstances affecting its culture. The lines of Modernism, thought stalled or blurred by social upheaval in the decade, continued to develop in the U.S. primarily in fiction, where Faulkner's analyses of the South constituted a final flowering of Modernist prose. At the heart of his experiments was a sense of the profound, archetypal past, a dimension of primitive rituals and mysteries which formed the base of Southern life and gave to Faulkner's characters and situations their peculiar power and universality. Hemingway's exploration of modern life, which, though sometimes clumsily romanticized, bore direct connection to the theories of the past developed in European Modernism. The descent in time was pursued differently by American writers, and occasioned many more excursions into the non-European past of Amerindian culture, or into the regional mysticism found in Robinson Jeffers and sometimes Steinbeck.

But a dichotomy was forming at the heart of Americian literature which did not become apparent until the 1940s. Political and social instability had encouraged various groups in the U.S. to more closely identify American writing with British tradition. The Agrarian movement of the 1930s openly espoused traditional prosody and English conventions; Southern regional life portrayed in its literature bore close resemblance to rural life in England. Beneath these mannerly parallels lay a more significant identification of race and religion: the Agrarians defined American literary tradition in terms of British continuities—a white Anglo-Saxon Protestant culture distinct from the mixed races and religions of the industrial northeast. Britain signified a racial and religious purity that included only a small portion of the U.S. population. Eliot's retrenchment to cultural and religious orthodoxy provided the intellectual leadership to guide the Southern movement whose attitudes were becoming widely disseminated through academic channels. Up to the 1950s, an entrenced British loyalty reigned supreme in American education.

Olson seized on an alternative cultural tradition in the native civilizations crushed by the Spanish expansion into the New York from the south. In *The Maximus Poems* he focused on the town of Gloucester as a victim of the British expansion from the north. The native life that was conquered left only the rubble of its ideas and languages, whose fragments make up a sufficient metaphor of a past lying outside contemporary reality. The temples and villages lay buried underneath modern corrupted Mexico, as reported in "The Kingfishers," where the once sacred quetzal feathers are no longer wanted or exported and where "the pool is slime." So are the buried foundations of the old fishing port at Cape Ann remnants below the modern sense of reality, part of the temporal and experiential underworld through which Maximus roams as his memory becomes "the history of time." All through the early Olson runs the same complaint that reality has shrunk to a pathetic egotism and a feverish concern for the supremacy of the white race and its narrow heritage of ideas and principles. The cramped boundaries of awareness he keeps pushing back obliquely convey his quarrel with Western racial supremacy, the Anglo-Saxon idealism rampant in the Truman years and the early days of the Cold War. The past beckoned, but the nation seemed frozen in panic, unable to deal with the opportunity of a new world order the war had proffered to it. As the first postmodernist, Olson was the most aware of the political crossroads at which the nation hesitated. The chance to establish a new relation to other cultures was fast receding as the government withdrew into the security of its armaments and its old cherished bonds to an island nation in the North Atlantic.

The course of postmodernism coincided with the fortunes of France's ex-colony, Vietnam. "President Franklin D. Roosevelt seems instinctively to have recognized that colonialism was doomed and that the United States must identify with the forces of nationalism in Asia," George Herring wrote in *America's Longest War*. "In 1945, however, Roosevelt retreated sharply from his earlier forthright stand in support of Indochinese independence" (5), and by 1947, under Truman's adminstration, the U.S. government abandoned its support of nationalist causes and became "increasingly obsessed with the Communist menace in Europe." Ho Chi Minh "had openly appealed for American support, even indicating that Indochina would be a 'fertile field for American capital and enterprise.'" But as George C. Marshall explained, the U.S. was unwilling to see "colonial empires and adminstrations supplanted by philosophies and political organizations emanating from the Kremlin" (*America's Longest War* 8). From the first independence war in Vietnam to the revolution in Cuba in 1959, American foreign policy followed a strategy of "containment" of Soviet expansion. Throughout the 1960s, the arts re-examined America's democratic ideals and held them up to government as a vision betrayed. "Ho's appeals for support" were "ignored," wrote Herring, even though his nation had adopted most of the text of America's own Constitution. Postmodern writers could only note the contradictions of American foreign policy as preparations for a new war in Vietnam got underway. They expressed their anger against the war policy by showing support for the colonial victims of imperial rivalry abroad and for racial and cultural minorities at home, whose plight they associated with the colonies abroad. In turning to the literature of the American Renaissance, Olson, a Roosevelt liberal, seemed to know it was the place to begin a critique of contemporary political vison. The genesis of national vision in the 1850s would come to haunt America's policy makers in the era of decolonization. In time, experimental literature honed its inquiry into the foundations of Anglo-Saxon thought, its fears, biases and obsessions.

Though the 1960s are taken up with the portrait of a rebel against his enemies, when Eshleman begins his journal "Heaven-Bands" in May, 1969, he resumes wrestling with the ambiguities of his "Indiana" theme. Other poets had gone another way than his, and Eshleman comes back to the question of religion. It has been a religious century, and Eshleman now found himself surrounded by a variety of complex spiritual issues: Snyder's Buddhism, Blackburn's Catholic inhibitions; Rothenberg's interest in Judaic mysticism and his Jewish roots; Ginsberg's religious maunderings and conversion to Buddhism. The Catholic emphasis of Black Mountain poetry, from Olson to Blackburn and Kelly (who later converted to Buddhism), now merged with the Catholic background of Vallejo, French surrealism, the tormented Catholic heritage that ran through European, Central and South American literature of the 20th century. But Eshleman was still running from the restraints of Presbyterianism at home, and was, in 1969, very much under the spell of Wilhelm Reich's sexual therapy.

Reich's mystical sense of a pure orgiastic freedom as redemption offered a potential poetic that might link up the "deep image" ideas. The orgasm was a form of descent to the underworld, where all distinctions and separations dissolved as one reeentered a primordial ecstasy of being. Each orgasm was a plunge to innocent pre-human freedom, a return to Eliade's notion of redemptive darkness, the regenerative abyss. But in "Heaven-Bands," Eshleman seems to have realized he had half a proposition in Reich, and another half in religion, which he still loathed:

> Temples, cathedrals, churches etc., are inhabitations
> of money-changers & the pitiful drugged majority of
> humanity. To call a place "holy" that is built like a great
> leech-work on the neck and backs of men for thousands
> of years! That place—the temple—which has as its
> primary reason for being its weekly anti-sex meetings—
> masses, services—

Western religion was the organized denial of sexual pleasure among its adherents; resistance to religious proscription formed the argument of *Indiana*. But now that he had a position regarding the value and importance of sexual freedom, he needed a foil in the church, whose condemnation of sexual pleasure he could debate. Just after his mother's death, he wrote "I have tested my crowbars / against your form —

I have broken your given
   image—mother
father—against you, with &
   beyond you my understanding
of world—which is poetry—
   is tried in fire—it holds—
neither pure nor impure.

And in a letter to Ken Irby, Eshleman remarked that his intention as a poet was "to help men & women to mobilize their energies—that is ALWAYS THE POINT, TO GET AT THE AUTHENTIC ENERGIES AND GET THEM INTO UTTERANCE." He later wrote, "I wanted a poem, then, that would trace my spiritual evolution in one poem from the time I married in 1961 thru the phases of my evolution to, then 1966—how the *form* of woman had constantly changed yet remained a constant—that my life had taken several discernible 'turns' from an ignorant innocence to . . . how each [woman] had, in experience, helped me clarify what creation was." That poem was "The Physical Traveler" published in *Coils*. But it could not be written in 1966; in *Coils*, the date given is Lima, 1966–Sherman Oaks, 1972. The poem "Coils" makes a firm declaration of sexual vision as the final leap to freedom from his troubled youth. Now "Eros" was the "push outward, is behind Sex and thru Sex blossoms to include a fuller sense of love—." While Eshleman "was experiencing a rebirth" in Kyoto, he remarked in "Heaven-Bands," "Corman was there talking poetry all the time—but also with heavy death-preoccupation in his presence." As Eshleman worked on his Vallejo translations, he was fascinated by "his overpowering suppressed *force* tied in with constant death presence." The pieces of his essential drama were falling together finally: Vallejo was the suffering male whose desire for sexual freedom had been prevented, tormentingly distorted by Catholic heritage. Here was the parallel between them: both had suffered the crushing inhibitions of their religious cultures, and Vallejo had survived by renewing his indigenous roots, his adherence to Marxism, and by his creative struggle with Christianity. Vallejo's power lay in his destructive imbalance—a powerful nature held back, baffled, unable to connect with the Eros principle within him. And yet, it was this suffering that had reorganized reality into powerful visionary language, the distored images of which plumbed an Indian underworld.

In a way, Eshleman was trying to resolve the riddle of Vallejo's power during these crucial years in the early 1970s: great poetry involved both a suffering distortion of Eros and its possession by instinctual grasp.

> All poetry that is not complaint after the Neolithic is
> in service of the State— (1967—copied out of notebook,
> 12 Sept 71)

Religion was one arm of the state, according to the journal notes, the force creating civilization, such as it was, the extreme it was driven to by the denial of sexual freedom. Religion was the gate shut against descent to primordial unity, the motion backward toward human origin. Civilization was a current running *away* from human source, which religion reinforced by its denunciation of the body. "Unrelenting boredom: the Catholic heritage."

> Church perfect metaphor for state of Mexican soul—
> fort architecture without imagination, big dumb brick
> and stone BOX.

"God, why must man forever hold up something as corny, as lethal, as Catholic rite? Why must he adore Virginity as that which denies *him*—isn't the real mystery that a woman remains fresh fucked again and again?" "Destroy all religious systems."

Eshleman could only repeat his conclusion that religion

was the grid of ideas holding back anyone's effort to discover his or her true nature; through sexual freedom alone could one return to the center of nature. But in an interview in the late 1970s, Eshleman remarked that his interest in Vallejo sprange from his "unique combination of sources," "the Indian, the Christian, and the Marxist, . . . with the Christian emphasis probably the most beguiling."

> In 1963 I was only beginning to imagine my personal background which was shaped by a Presbyterian reading of the Bible. There was a part of my personality that wanted to be the ultimate Christian and the first Vallejo poem that really, as they say, hooked me, suffers the condition of wanting to be Jesus but of not *being* Jesus. My hitch-hiking down to Mexico twice, in 1957 and 1958, introduced me to Indian and Spanish-American culture, which immediately told me how narrow my own WASP ledge in the world was.

Of James Wright's poetry, Eshleman remarked, his "most interesting work is the writing of a suffering Protestant *denied imagination*" [my emphasis]. Eshleman then concluded with this intriguing judgment:

> Many major European and Latin American poets come out of Catholic backgrounds; very few major North American poets do. I suspect that this may be a more significant distinction than whatever Bly means by unity and identity. Most of us have a Protestant unconscious, and since Protestantism eliminated purgatory, or limbo, a long time ago, this suggests that we have less access to the pagan world, or to a polytheism, than European and Latin American poets with their possibly more rich *and* resistant religious backgrounds. Religiously speaking, they meet more prohibitions than we do, and this in turn stimulates a more aggressive form of transgression.

188

Catholicism's morbid preoccupation with sin had kept alive a vision of primordial life, vividly and compellingly in literature, art, and architecture. Though it condemned erotic freedom, it preserved the powers of Eros in rituals and iconography, and by some ineffable logic actually fed on the memory of primordial eroticism.

To sin was to go backward toward origins; "original sin," Eshleman remarked in "Trenches" (in *Coils*), was the "limit of the fall," the final abyss. Hell was the point at which human identity dissolved into the animal continuum, where devils wore tails, and sinners, in the delirious visions of Hieronymous Bosch, crumbled into monstrous deformities, half-human, half-animal. Hell was the twilight world of proto-human forms, sphinxes, centaurs, mermen, gorgons, a realm of imagination in which animal forms ignored human fulfillment.

"The passing of a psyche into new form" required a shift from one theological tradition, the Protestant axis, to another, the Catholic tradition, not by conversion or leap of faith, but through the inroads of translations, in which one figuratively became the poet of that tradition, mouthing another's words and tincturing them with one's own personality. In effect, translation was a form of conversion, without the commitment to the actual dogma; Eshleman wished to be near the animating vision that contained the echoes and residues of primordial memory, which only Catholic writers possessed sufficiently. The creative Catholic intelligence was still generalized, frozen at a point of evolution, interfaced with modernity on one side and spiritual antiquity on the other, an awareness fraught with curious chthonic gods and powers and a modern empirical orientation. The Catholic writer distorted experience from just the tilt of his own paradoxical consciousness, in which literary realism melted into allegory, parables, supernaturalism, mythical episodes, gnostic literature, or what has recently been described as metafiction. The world-wide reversals of realistic writing in the late 20th century might well be considered the effect of the influence of hispanic Catholic culture, with its powerful appeals to myth and fabula, to which the canons of Protestant secular realism have given in.

Eshleman had immersed himself in translation work in the early 1970s, and his collaborative translation of Vallejo's *Spain, Take this Cup from Me* appeared in 1974; his translations of Antonin Artaud's *Letter to André Breton* (1974) and *To Have Done with the Judgment of God* (1975) were followed a year later by *Artaud the Mômo;* in 1978 appeared Vallejo's *Battles in Spain,* followed in 1978 by the culmination of his long preoccupation with Vallejo, *The Complete Posthumous Poetry,* in collaboration with José Rubia Barcia. These efforts constitute Eshleman's explorations of two spheres of imagination within the Catholic heritage, two expansions of vision, the one into racial identity and a realm of intermingled Christian and Peruvian Indian sensibility, the other, a violent moral and esthetic upheavel, the profound "transgression" which, as Eshleman had put it, the inhibitions of Catholicism goaded from its writers. The translations thus figure in the canon as primary texts: the visionary odysseys of Vallejo, Artaud, Césaire, and others expand his own theme of transforming psyche, of burrowing into the layers of one's heritage to find a new identity closer to the core of imagination.

In 1974, Eshleman read Mikhail Bakhtin's *Rabelais and His World* in which Bakhtin showed medieval Western life plunging below Greek time into primordial unconsciousness, a mental state prior to the conscious life of *civilization.* Though he does not specify its exact location in time or space, this realm extends into the lower body, whose mockery of the day-world is complete and devastating, and which expressed itself through what Bakhtin calls "carnival laughter." Throughout the old agricultural calendar of festivals, which medieval Europe still observed, towns and villages made a ritual descent into this realm—and vented the frustrations and rages of the psyche against order and rationality. The celebrants wore animal disguises, danced wildly in drunken processions, and relived the Dionysian orgies of early Greece, as they took apart the order of their conscious world for a day or two of abandoned revelry. In effect, the dream state had been dredged up into reality, and the whole force of unconscious energy unleashed on authority and hierarchy, often violently. The law was put in abeyance, and the town fathers looked away as this purgative ritual played itself out.

For Bakhtin, this was the healthful anarchy of the ancient world lingering in Europe in its last days. The humor of that revelry was conveyed intact in the grotesque imagination of Rabelais, with his rich imagery of excretion, deformity, vomiting, and wounds. These are the tributaries of the gut and the lower functions, venting repression from all the points of the human organism. It was a flushing and drenching of the waking body of its buried, repressed soul.

What Eshleman saw in Bakhtin he had seen elsewhere in the paintings of Soutine, whose studies of animal flesh are a kind of dreamwork on the facticity of life, in the tormented poetry and prose of Artaud, and certainly in Hillman, whose sense of therapy involves the reclaiming of this sleep-imagination as the soul-mate of waking, which Bakhtin saw exposed in medieval revelry and in Rabelais. The concern with dreams, with *depth* itself "leads us," Hillman writes,

> . . . to pay special attention to *whatever is below*. This has been so since the beginning of psychoanalysis, and its notion of suppression, subconscious, and shadow. These are terms for what we see in images: burials, the dead, ancestors; workers in refuse, sewers, plumbers; criminals and outcasts; the lower body, its garments and

its functions; lower forms of life that we 'look down
upon,' from apes to bugs; the underside of the world,
the floor of the sea, the downstairs and cellars, and,
in fact anything whatsoever that can be turned over
in the sense of *hyponoia* to revel a deeper significance.

(139)

The only difference between Hillman's view of free-
ing the lower self and Bakhtin's is in the emotion each feels
accompanies the process: for Bakhtin, laughter is at the
depths of the psyche, and is the psyche's own voice mocking the dayworld; for Hillman, there is a *tristesse* involved
in this eruption of the human underworld:

> . . . The emotions that go with these images of bottom-
> ing are reluctance, loathing, sadness, mourning,
> enclosure, lethargy, or that sense of depth that presses
> on us as depression, oppression, suppression. Our
> downward imagination has entered the earth. Bottom's
> dream.

(139–40)

If we add the sexual premises of Wilhelm Reich to the
sense of underworld defined by Hillman and Bakhtin, we
begin to puzzle out the meaning of Eshleman's own underworld in the poetry he began writing after *The Gull Wall*.
Though he had not read Hillman yet, already he had approached him through Norman O. Brown's *Life Against
Death: The Psychoanalytical Meaning of History* (1959), in
which a similar argument is made on the relation of death
(psyche) and the healthy consciousness. Brown traces the
meanings of excrement in vision and psychic life in "Studies
in Anality," which Hillman draws on in his own discussion
of "Mud and Diarrhea," in *The Dream and the Underworld*
(184). Both Hillman and Brown arrive at the same conclusion, that at the heart of death in the underworld lay
Eros, the remaking of relations that death makes possible.

Love begins when the independent fictions of consciousness are broken down, their souls exposed and linked to one another through the medium of psychic images, the dream. Here is Hillman's version of the process:

> . . . this formative imaginative work is always at the same time deformative, destructive. Each approach to the underworld is through Styx and must meet the obstacle of its hateful coldness. This is unavoidable and cannot be sentimentalized. Every correct move in this nightworld kills what it touches . . . [but] by bringing an image close to death, concurrently makes it live again.
>
> (130)

For Brown (and for Hillman) Christianity prevented the two processes of the soul, life and death, from maintaining a healthful dialectic of construction/destruction of the world. For both writers, and for Eshleman, Christianity drove the psyche from awareness, and sealed off all channels leading down into a realm of death and reconstitution below. As Hillman writes, "The victory over sleep and death is part of Christianism's larger mission that exchanges soul for spirit" (87). Brown puts the issue more polemically.

> The time has come to ask Christian theologians, especially the neo-orthodox, what they mean by the resurrection of the body and by eternal life. Is this a promise of immortality after death? In other words, is the psychological premise of Christianity the impossibility of reconciling life and death either in "this" world or the "next," so that flight from death—with all its morbid consequences—is our eternal fate in "this world" and in "the next"?
>
> (308)

Eshleman's first trip to the caves of the Dordogne in 1974 coincides with his reading of Bakhtin; perhaps the whole array of his reading was galvanized into vision with the experience of the caves, some of which he returned to repeatedly to study the wall paintings. Hillman had already completed the short first version of *The Dream and the Underworld,* which appeared in the *Eranos Yearbook*-42 in 1973; Eshleman was putting his own similar theory of the caves together a year later, and read the essay version of "The Dream and the Underworld" in 1978 before he returned to the Dordogne a second time. When he did, he discovered an underworld in actuality, a labyrinth in which paleolithic humanity daubed and slashed their marks, their primordial psychic images. For Eshleman, the markings were a first language in the world, the primal separation between waking and sleep, between the hadic darkness of imagination and preliminary consciousness.

With this thesis, he could ground the whole of his poetry and give it the mythopoeic center needed to draw its various themes of exploration, maturity, and struggle into a coherent argument. With *Hades in Manganese* (1981), he began work on the meaning of image itself. The caves were both metaphor and fact at once, a *place* of dark and labyrinthine complexity that may have given us the original trope for soul as *within, below,* buried deep in self, as an *earth* within self, which hoarded all of its pure images, its archetypes of the sleepworld. The cave markings, he tells us in the Preface, elaborated over thousands of years, constitute "a history of image," a record of the struggle to invent a means for transposing the infinite dreamworld onto stone. Remarkably, Schwerner's *The Tablets* sets out to record the very same moment, though from the vantage point of already written documents, the Sumero-Akkadian "tablets" which have since come to represent the first linguistic system of Mesopotamian culture. But Schwerner is wholly in agreement with Eshleman's intentions—to show the hesitant, problematic nature of fixing the living mind's content into a two-dimensional record of any kind. *The Tablets* are as much about the angst of "birth" and "waking" as are Eshleman's poems on the cave-exile theme.

We are never sure with Eshleman where metaphor and fact separate as he explores his thesis about the caves. Sometimes he thinks of the caves as the rocky enclosures of mind itself, the earth dreaming its images to itself; from that angle, paleolithic humanity was the thief of image who tore it out of the earth's own psyche (the Promethean myth of image as stolen from chthonic earth gods) to replicate as the language of *human* consciousness. This version of Image is worked out in the long poem "Visions of the Fathers of Lascaux." From another perspective, the caves are the theater in which the tragedy of humanity was enacted; the exile from Edenic sleep occurs the moment a single image is wrested from within, the Platonic tragedy, and faultily transposed onto stone by means of pigments, excrement, the hacking of quartz against limestone—as consciousness sprang into being and accepted the shadows of reality as its awareness. From those shadows in the limestone theater of illusion also sprang up the notion of a purely sterile death, a vacant underworld of mere terminations of things, instead of the great centrifuge of actual Hades. Mortality and image were inseparable dimensions of a consciousness divorced from earth's own mind.

As Eshleman presents it, the birth of image marks the expulsion from Paradise; the image is, in Genesis terms, the first apple, the first fruit of human separation, a waking from the hadic dream state. The humanly transcribed image could only evolve toward increasing abstractness and formality, leaving the night-world further and further behind as it invented consciousness.

In "The Lich Gate," which opens *Hades in Manganese,*

the problem is how to announce all of these themes of descent, genesis, and expulsion that form the plot of the book. Eshleman has Hillman firmly in mind in the Preface as he tells us he will attempt to decode the cave walls the same way Hillman decodes dreams: as a language of psyche and the sleep-world, and not as "a reflection of daylight and daytime activity." A lich gate is the covered gate leading into a churchyard, where the bier awaits the clergyman for burial. "Lich" or "lych" is Middle English for the body, alive or dead, thus the gate is the passage out of life into death, the way down into psyche; the gate is also a kind of stone womb, the cave entrance itself where the body waits. Eshleman sees himself in both contexts: the past lies beyond the gate, the dead coming awake in what Hillman calls the "soul's *memoria*"; beyond death is a second life, the upside down world of the soul where everything is vital image. When Hillman remarks that sleep is an "initiation" into death, we may regard "The Lich Gate" as an initiation rite of descent. The meditation itself is a breathless congealing of memories and fantasized perceptions as he observes that the clergyman is Hades himself accompanied by "the dead who come forth to pull" his casket into the underworld. "I have come here," he says, "to make my language fray," to regain the image/ metaphor world of death, the soul's medium of ambiguous vitality.

Sleep and dreaming are, in Hillman's phrase, "soul-making" activities. They recapture the devitalized facts of ego and return them to the waters of underworld imagination. Eshleman presents us with the curious image of a persona waiting in his casket for burial, descent—from which we begin this journey into imagination. And it is a descent *into* the mind. The cave walls are like a mirror, and mirror images abound in this book. The pigmented figures, the dots, lines, and smudges making up the wall, are a consciousness that had worked itself up out of the interior rock, the mind

196

in nature; the person now looking at these images is the reverse of that genesis, the creature that was spawned and then liberated into the world. The cave wall is that pond we met in the beginning of *What She Means,* the reflecting surface that devoured the "i" of the figure gazing into it. Now we have a cave mirror in which the modern consciousness looks at images made *from the other side,* from the mind in stone, the earthly womb that gave birth to human consciousness. Thus the epigraph to *Hades*:

> A tentacle man dreaming in stone, of stone,
> pregnant, falling line looped forward,
> meandering out to
>
>   to—
>
>   to—
>
> a dot. But on its other side his tentacle
> remains detached, mirroring my fingertip,
>
>   my point,
>
> sound trace and twin . . .

The painted surface of the caves, the painted hadic underworld, in other words, is a line separating the two directions of human evolution: and the interface is an image seen—Eshleman has us imagine—from two sides: the eyes or mind in nature staring out, and the human and detached intellect, alien to nature, staring in. The caves are a looking glass, a pool, and by consequence, everything *behind* the rock surface is in reverse. This conception of psychic experience as the mirror-reverse of consciousness and the dayworld is also noted in *The Dream and the Under-world,* when Hillman points out that

> . . . Already then the dayworld and the nightworld, the
> two sides of the romantic soul, were conceived in a
> geographical theology of upperworld and netherworld.
> In "this theology," [Hillman is quoting from F. Cumont's
> *After Life in Roman Paganism* (New York: Dover
> Press, 1959)] "the world is divided into two halves by
> the line of the horizon; the upper hemisphere is the do-
> main of the living and the higher gods, the lower that
> of the dead and the infernal gods." The Egyptians had
> carried into extreme detail this reversed world below
> our feet. The dead walked upside down, feet up, heads
> down. "People there walk with their feet against the
> ceiling. This has the unpleasant consequence that diges-
> tion goes in the reverse direction, so that excrements
> arrive in the mouth."

Hillman drives home the point of reversal by noting that
"What is merely shit from the daytime perspective—or what
Freud called day-residues—becomes soul food when turned
upside down" (39).

The nightworld's retrogressions and reversals are the
only path to origins; its very steps of descent take one
backward in time, into the anti-mind of the brain. Eshleman
will point out as he fleshes his own vision of Hades in the
caves that the images were drawn in pigments made from
urine and vegetable dyes; the "shit" of the dayworld thus
became the soul-making images of the nightworld literally.
And in *Fracture,* he amplifies this idea in his narrative of
a patient who put his feces around the head of a sleeping
roommate—thus adorning the night-dreaming intellect with
the fecal amulets to be transmogrified. In a sense, the patient was helping to feed the imagination in its hadic descent.

But the nightworld's reversals of logic and awareness
come into play in Eshleman's new poetry with a deeper purpose. Descent to mental underworlds is another version of
Reichian release—the lower body erupts into the daylight

and releases the traumatic impactions that have robbed self of its sensitivity. Thus, descent brings up the old (indigestible?) food of the soul—in glutinous phraseology, in monotonous adjectival chains and syntactical clots, as if language itself were the fecal sediments drawn up by walking backward into hell, with feet on the ceilng. It is a language shaped in the coils of the gut forced out by descent. To stare at the imagery in the Dordogne caves is to go backward and throw up the past, like an Alice tumbling down the shaft, shrinking mysteriously as she descends to the floor of Wonderland, i.e., the unconscious.

> Self-purgatorial in a cunt hexed mirror
> he wandered off—"Come back!" the meadow
> in the mirror kept calling, where he had not
> seen his face but an otherness, in folds,
> Niaux, a huge cave had opened up
> where he was standing, but he didn't fall,
> for he was already at the bottom of a shaft,
> obsidian, and above? Floors of floor
> lamps, all turned on, since outside the store
> it was perpetually raining.
> The air was encysted with Freudian shapes,
> the life had been taken from bowl, or pen,
> the earth so long denied now turned its green
> feelers in, prefabricated yang and yin,
> but from where did the energy come that kept
> him in such purgatory? There, he knew the sun
> would always be, active in his mind, no more
> than floors of floor lamps lit, haloed by rain,
> which stood for universe, one switch,
> an apocalyptic purgatory in which the childhood
> elevator swam, and the water lights
> were always a thickness away, so that a meadow
> could beam through, but be immediately chastened,
> reduced to that vexed sore point in his palm.

"A Muscular Man with Gossamer Ways" (*HM* 19)

There are some interesting parallels between the imaginary landscape of Alice's underworld and that of Eshleman's. The animated figures of the chessboard, the tale of the Jabberwocky as a satire on the dayworld's male heroes—the grotesque animism of talking flowers, all have their equivalent in Eshleman's cartoon grotesques here (and later in *Fracture* and *Hotel Cro-Magnon*). In the Dordogne are looking-glass caves, and Eshleman cleverly establishes the dayworld as the artificial light of a department store's floor lamps, a memory from childhood. The meadow that beams "chastened" is once again the Butler Woods, and the window at 4705 Boulevard Place another mirror, an early image of the nightworld prefiguring the cave paintings he is now staring into, *with the same emotions.* "It was all / too complicated," says his adult persona, "—nature seemed to mean: / *go through,* but before him the cluster of stop / eat yield and loan signs sent neon shivers / into the most distant spore."

Déjà vu? Literally. Eshleman is bringing the 20th century right back to the rear door of the 19th, to the foreground of the Decadence and the early symbolist movement in Paris, to the world according to those artists, musicians, painters and poets Roger Shattuck describes in *The Banquet Years.* Indeed, he too must coin the term of a "mirrored realm" to get at the peculiar self-reflexiveness of the arts then, as we must now.

> Through self-reflexiveness, through concentration upon its own mobility and immobility, the artistic consciousness can shrink from the world into its own mirrored realm. . . . It is as if, in Edmund Wilson's terms, Axel and Rimbaud could inhabit a single human being who retreats from reality by seizing it in a sustained effort of transformation.
>
> . . . When the distinctions of art and reality have broken down, we are ourselves incorporated into the

structure of a work of art. Its very *form* importunes us to enter an expanded community of creation which now includes artist and spectator, art and reality.

We are once more in the '90s of a century, and the issue of interiority is again urged on us as a neglected area of intellect and awareness, a place to withdraw into to renew, bring about spiritual rebirth, to overcome the sense of aging and brittleness that an aging century induces in a civilization.

Infinite regression is that curious phenomenon of seeing oneself replicated in exactly facing mirrors as the images shrink in size toward the point of oblivion. All this is ready-made psychological language for Hillman and Eshleman. Eshleman keeps deriving new metaphors of this mirror realm, this reversed reality; the word "shaft" comes to represent both the corridors of the caves and the tunneling in toward the mirror world *behind* the image. Any image is now the mirror membrane separating the "two sides of the romantic soul":

> I am fused to the inability to
> reproduce what does determine me
> with its unborn baby hand
> which I finally learned to wear as earring in
> the Galapagos Trench pressure
> outside within what our species has lived.

(HM 25)

This is Frida Kahlo speaking in the poem "Frida Kahlo's Release"; Kahlo, a Mexican painter, was married to Diego Rivera, the celebrated muralist. She is now Eshleman's persona in another view of the painted image—the concept of image as being painted *from the other side* of the canvas, drawn by the "unborn" hand of the soul, whose access to the dayworld is sealed as tightly as is the hadic underworld of the dead. It is unborn, and it can only paint in reverse of what the dayworld sees. This poem anticipates another concept of Hillman's in a subsequent study in psychological theory, *Healing Fiction* (1983), when he remarks in his chapter on Alfred Adler, the Austrian psychiatrist, that the principal question of life is to ask, "What does the soul want?" It can only respond through the wounds inflicted on it by the dayworld's activities, the frustrations and repressions that slash at its hermetic innerworld and draw the blood of language up into consciousness. Wounds, therefore, such as Kahlo's impalement at fifteen on a metal bar in a street car accident, are the Adlerian vents through which the hand of the soul painted images the waking Kahlo recorded as her nightside:

> Out of the cave of inner nurture,
> where animal conception could have been,
> I connected my muzzle
> beam to my snout post.
> Gamy iodine on a silver plate,
> I transformed the hospital linen
> into more than a daguerrotype of paradise.

It is another use of the "shaft," which penetrates from all sides into the unconscious, and will ultimately come to signify the shaft of the phallus penetrating the uterine-cave of the female. Hence, the poem "Maithuna," in *Fracture* (120), where the special sense of a trance/descent is felt after intercourse.

What we are learning to accept in *Hades* is the world under the image screen, the reversed world of the soul, whose language is the dying out of conscious literalism and the emergence of the fused, entangled, dream-laden lyricism from the other side. A trope of the poem itself is emerging throughout the last three books of his canon—the idea that we are ourselves, the readers, looking down on the pond-surface of Eshleman's poetry, at a cave/mirror/shaft page whose inscriptions are given to us by the poet's own unborn hand reaching up from below. Remember how we are introduced to the poet in "Lich Gate": he is *dead,* waiting to be buried behind the mirror of awareness from which to talk to us. Only then, behind the membrane of image, can he give vent to the soul, and let tumble out of the mouth all the blood of the wounded soul he now embodies. The last poem of *Hades,* "The Shaft," brings all this home to a point, as does "Cimmeria" just before it. In "The Shaft," "the dead nourishes the living," and we are back to the dream in the poem "The Gull Wall" (*TGW* 37), where Eshleman *joins* the dead Blackburn and helps him negotiate the labyrinth of the underworld, where he will heal himself. Now we have the image of the relation between upper and lower worlds, conscious and unconscious; each nourishes the other in the balanced life. And in "Cimmeria," we have this variation (frequently worked in Eshleman's poetry) on a line from Wallace Stevens' "The Snowman," where Eshleman writes, "One must have a mind of stone / to find lineage in cave scrapes meandering, / and to have been uprooted, /   / for a long time, to express ligament / stalagmite to Auschwitz." One must be able to *die* to speak for the soul, to slip into trances and go behind the screen of consciousness to find the link between one's own "dead" self and the great dead in their separate realm.

It's here we can glimpse the political axis of his new poetry, and find the imperialist critique about to surface: the so-called "backward" people of the earth, the "undeveloped" nations, are themselves behind the image screen, below the dayworld's imagery, as read by a superpower's will and ambitions. The Third World is a third state of mind, close to the soul's language, partially submerged in the shaft of "otherness." The war between mental worlds fought out in the American psyche has its outward manifestation in the desire to destroy the part of humanity who represent the "unborn" double, the mirrored twin of self. Hence, Eshleman's tirades against American aggression in Vietnam, in Central America, Africa, against minorities, against any sense of "backward," which in the new terminology of these poems turns out to be soul-speech, the deep psyche's culture. A whole moral/ethical system of the verse will be deduced from this mirror polarity developing in *Hades*: what we see in the mirror, the Thou looking back from inside the mirror's shaft, is the loathed soul protected by its stygian waters. What Prufrock also saw in his own mirror as he dressed his conscious self with such hopeless resignation, cut off from woman and true sleep, left to a life in the dayworld. The soul inhabited "otherness," and the desire to literalize, capture, and name all the things of waking existence required that the soul be driven out of mind.

Eshleman wants us to believe that this descent into Hades is a healing journey, the very one mapped out by Hillman's books. This encounter with death and the soul-realm is meant to overcome what Norman O. Brown characterizes as the disabling opposition between life and death. The figure in the casket in "Lich Gate" is a patient waiting for the minister/doctor to take him under and restore to his mind the hemisphere of the lower world. That involves relinking self to all the alien dimensions of self, lower body, lower realms of world culture, the lower/darker world of the feminine—the shaft down which a long succession of female lovers from Persephone to Eurydice have descended to become brides of Hades.

"O dead living depths!" cries the voice in the title poem, "Hades in Manganese." Now Eshleman can *re*translate hero myths as chapters in the epic war against the soul. Hence,

> Perseus holds the written head out to the sun.
> His sword from his hip projects what is on his mind,
> a center torn from a center, Medusa

wrenched from her jellyfish stronghold,
her severed pipes, the caterwauling serpents,
his treasure from the underworld.

This is the male archetype again, the Western ego pitting all his consciousness against the terrors of the deep, the horrified underworld.

The hero will not be
transfixed into himself, he will lift
reflected terror from reflected depth,
he will thrust his hand down
into the sodden tampax mass where earth bleeds.

The passage is a skillful manipulation of his basic themes, the male ego in conflict with the female soul, the shaft turned uterus, a bleeding orifice of the lower body from which this Medusa head has been pulled. The Medusa herself is the soul's own face made unbearably terrifying to the male mind. She is every dragon and monster, every Jabberwocky and "gook" hiding in the dark and driven out in the psychomachia of Western literature. Eshleman turns this mythic subject directly into personal history again by making Perseus once more his own father at the slaughterhouse:

My father, for thirty years timing blacks
slaughtering steers, folds into men
beating the animal in other men,
extracting Pan-pipes, jugular flutes of morning.

The horizon line between two realities is now redrawn and Eshleman pulls his whole argument together when he notes that

Surface is reality as is ascension
as is depth. Medusa hangs down through
fathoms of archaic familiarity,
the pylons men have made of female psyche,
women beat into gates through which to draw

the ore of heroic energy, to appease
a masculine weather for manipulation and torture.

Ascension brings us back to Christ, who conquers the underworld and death and thus obviates the soul's own ground. Its image-base is replaced by the abstractness of heaven. Hence, Lazarus is someone we regard as having been delivered out of death for perpetual life, i.e., everlasting waking—the male's way of redemtion. One birth is enough, one "gate" out of the feminine underworld and a destiny linked with the sun and sky. The very name Blackburn is a kind of encrypted metaphor of a Christian inferno, the Catholic hell of heat without light. Even so, Eshleman is not as opposed to the Catholic vision as Hillman is, who rejects the whole system of Christian symbolism of hell. Eshleman seems intrigued with the notion that Catholics are still linked with the underworld by means of the obsession with hell and damnation, with the traces of animism in certain branches of Third World Catholic belief. Hence, the dreams of rescuing or encountering poets in a Dantean Inferno, such as in the Blackburn dream poems and again in "At the Speed of Wine," in *Hotel Cro-Magnon,* where we meet the drowned Hart Crane, with whom Eshleman has a very Dantean conversation:

> "Poets in death need poets in life," [Crane] sobbed,
> "not parasitically, my dear wench,
> we need you here, under the image mill,
> where Samson's soles are a kind of liquor for our eyes,
> here, in the emptiness of the North American
>   underworld,
> any image you twist through the wringer of pubescent
>   lubricity, tensioned on sheer need,
> is manna to us,
> no image = no food, as simple as that!

> (*HCM* 144)

These and similar passages scattered all through the later poetry suggest the point at which Hillman and Eshleman part. Eshleman is more sensitive, as a poet, to the literature of the Christian era that *uses* and explores a fruitful sense of hell despite its negation by theology. Indeed, Hillman is silent on the wealth of this post-Greek imaginative literature, from *The Confessions,* to the rich lode of work on the temptations of St. Anthony (and other saints), to Dante, Tasso, the Romantic canon, and the Catholic poets Eshleman has translated. Hillman's conception of the soul is that its voices are the polytheistic pantheon of paganism, which Christianity destroyed. Hence, psychotherapy's own vision cannot accept the versions of underworlds of the Christian era because they are by definition monotheistic. But even so, the gods return—even in horrific form—to writers of the post-Greek world, and Eshleman deploys both Hillman's vision and his own; where they disagree, he goes his own way.

What we are tracing is a new *via negativa* in the cave poetry; all the elements were present in the prior books, but they were unassembled, treated in isolation. Now, Eshleman has an epic sense of his theme and he brings into the poetry a variety of epic narrative conventions to introduce his story of the healing journey to the underworld. In his Introduction to *Fracture,* book two of his descent narrative, we have an initiation tale serving as proem in which several incidents coalesce into a death vision: hunting the French *cèpes* or wild mushrooms, finding some of what he had harvested were *faux cèpes,* a false variety which "when pressed firmly bruise blue, and are poisonous"; the sight of giant slugs "vibrating on their backs," whether "in agony or in ecstasy," he couldn't tell. These omens are followed by the "fatal" incident, a sprained ankle while crawling through a cave; later, driving home after a dinner where his host points out a "devil's mask" hung on the wall, a spasm seizes the "left

calf," and his car is hurtled into a ditch opposite a ravine
"that we later found out was the graveyard of several tourist
cars per year." The ankle was broken in three places, hence
the title *Fracture* of the volume. We are well prepared for
our second, and deeper descent into Eshleman's underworld.
After the accident, he tries to "make sense out of what had
happened,"

> I thought back to when I had begun to write in
> 1958. Forces were breaking out like diseases, and for
> years I was beside myself with the midwestern hydra
> that had been unleashed. The main thing that kept me
> going was a belief that if I fully worked through the sex-
> ism, self-hate, bodilessness, soullessness, and suf-
> focated human relationship which encrusted my
> background, I could excavate a basement. I would have
> torn down the "House of Eshleman" and laid out a new
> foundation in its place. I feared that if I did not do this
> I would be hooked back into the hands of my selfhood
> by Indiana at the point that I was approaching a "last
> judgment" in my work.

(F 11–12)

The point is, we have not left Indiana behind; the
house he grew up in has returned once more to be destroyed,
dug down into and tunneled out of toward freedom. The
constancy of this image of Indiana—as the pole of conscious
self-disintegration, is an essential element of Eshleman's
poetic. This is a poetry of healing; its esthetic is not pleasure
or instruction but remediation, and therefore its patient must
be present in each lyrical frame, the poet himself. The ill-
ness can never be transcended, since the poetic has no
grounds for presenting the recuperated imagination. Each
book starts with the ailing, fractured self—whose partial
living-death is cause for self-examination, the violence of
therapy, or the descent/quest narrative. The healing process

of one book leads to the study of another wound, another source of spiritual fragmentation. In that way, the plot of the canon is a kind of spiraling outward over the same ground, a hovering over the same scene of childhood but from loftier perspectives and with greater maturity of vision each time we pass over the house at 4705 Boulevard Place, where the twelve-year old Clayton is continually reperceived in the progressively older poet's imagination. The child is the unalterable datum, now an image of the soul itself, staring out his window, mounting Sparkie the dog, drifting into a maligned puberty. Childhood itself is the diseased portion of memory, the wound that cannot heal.

The result is a poetry whose sense of closure is only narratological; the emotional content is inexhaustible because it emanates from the soul at some irrational level of awareness. These Adlerian descents into mind are raids on memory toward that topos of image where the child Clayton resides in its immutable death. Eshleman tells us in the Introduction that he is reminded of Diane Arbus' photograph of the "Jewish Giant," a pituitary giant stooping in his parents' house, as the metaphor of his own situation—the immensely impacted and frustrated youth/soul held captive in his imagination. Thus this picture of his own imago-self in "The Death of Bill Evans":

> Can't see the wound for the scars,
> a small boy composed of scabs is staring into
> the corner of his anatomy—where walls and floors end
> he figures he ends, so he wears his end
> like glasses before his eyes,
> beckoned into the snow he will be beaten
> by children he thought were his friends,
> the implication of his hurt is so dark
> it will scab over to be rescabbed the next time,
> and he will grow not by internal urge to mature

but by scabbings until, grown big, he will be the size
        of an adult
and his face will look like a pebbly gourd.
He will stay inside the little house I have built
        for him, in which to stand he must stoop.

(F 32)

The drama of healing has no fundamental advance; the act is always approximate, a treatment of the soul wound that engages language and dissipates its motive lyric by lyric down through the voluminous output of his writing. The vastness of the work is one dimension of its poetic—the obsession with an unending process whose accumulation is not a progress toward any goal, but rather an activity unto itself, its only task. The poems are therefore quite the opposite of the traditional or conventional poem; these are not wrestlings with the irrational made sensible, brought up to light. These descents bring up no underworld treasure, no stolen wisdom to the dayworld. Instead, these poems are waking dreams, the daily encounter with altered imaginal states of mind, whose content whelms up out of the hurt soul but do not build an edifice of dream content in which to consciously live. Instead, just as he says in the Introduction, these forays into the death/dream world of image are to glimpse the self's embryonic form, the soul in its serene burial ground, which enables the poet to take down the dayworld edifice built by his parents and by midwestern culture. The healing is a continual destruction of the ego, but not a building up of the soul from death, only its enlarging presence within the house (of words) he has contructed as its shrine.

If a progress does ensue in these books leading up to *Fracture* and beyond, it is one of balance, counterpoint, a strengthening dialectic in the self's preparation for death, the essence of Hillman's definition of psychotherapy. The soul-work of imagination is only an initiation into the final descent, which these poems lay out in a spiraling meditation over *birth*.

Thus, any of the dream structures we encounter in *Fracture* are variations on the principal dream of self; what happens in the paleolithic schism of the caves, that moment of separation from the earth and of human exile in consciousness, is a way of dreaming his own birth, his own traumatic maturation into a daylight ego cut off from passion and true depth. "Visions of the Fathers of Lascaux," the central poem of this collection, is a narrative of the birth of the species, but it is also his own birth, his own coming into the literal world through the hacking of stone and the daubing of moist limestone wall. The real trauma of birth is the loss of imagination, the leaving behind of the watery underside of image, where relation is infinite and eternal.

The cave as metaphor of underworld is one way in which to make descent more accessible; the Dordogne is strewn with such caverns where the imagination of early human existence is recorded, and whose entryways are open, accessible, indeed, waiting for any curious tourist to buy his ticket and explore. Used this way, the cave is a new conception of mind and its dream states, and perfectly fits its intended use in these poems. It does not challenge us to question the accuracy of Eshleman's hypothesis; that is almost beside the point. The important thing is the metaphor itself, its generality as a sign of unconscious access, its use of a place of artistic composition at the childhood of the species. In "The Loaded Sleeve of Hades" (*F* 34–36), we find Eshleman taking on the voice of a scolding tour guide, leading us (the tourists and his own waking self) through a cave and explaining in impatient tones how we have stumbled into our own minds, our own evolutionary labyrinths. This Dantean guide speaks *for* the underworld, and chides us for our literal expectations down in the moist depths of the soul:

> And did you know that caves are warehouses
> in which ghosts of winds that first
> investigated Pre-Cambrian earth
> are also stored, so that Les Trois Frères,
> coiled in tattooed splendor,
> molecularly licking, still today,
> its paleolithic wounds, is affectionate,
> exuberant and lethal all at once—
> there is, thus, through you,
> a tunnel that winds back into total discontinuity
> which you tried to conceal
> with the innocence that taking on the underworld
> would not have repercussions

Eshleman writes now as an initiate of these caves, someone almost on the *other* side of the wall, even as he addresses himself—as the naif who has wandered too far. He tells us of similar warnings (cf. Introduction) of the dangers of invoking the underworld and the archetypes of mind by a yogi and by Hillman himself, but now he is the warning voice against his own excursions into death. "Rhapsody" has this new tone of familiarity with the underworld as he talks to his wife, who now drives him around with his broken ankle in a cast:

> As you drove me about, at 25 miles per hour,
> through transomed halls of trees,
> I have never been closer to green,
> to its lifting majestic detours,
> the way, when it relaxes, it is garbage,
> a fresh death, my quiet lust to not move,
> as if I emerged only to experience
> how still I am,
> how only as a foetus
> was I rooted in true velocity.

(F 39)

Eshleman's view of the soul as an integrity that un-
wound itself into self *and* soul makes the cave into a kind
of psychological centrifuge, an image he works on in "Notes
on a Visit to Le Tuc D'Audoubert" (*F* 46–52), which combines prose, verse, and ink sketches of various cave-wall
figures. There he seizes on the shape of the cave itself as
"image turbine," a tunnel twisting in the earth where the
halves of the soul came apart in various stages. And he can
trace through certain other ideas—the sorcerer as the first
human figure to emerge from death, the prototype of
Hermes-Mercurius, whose wisdom is the vestiges of underworld memory.

The task is to imagine the process by which image leapt
from the underworld into life, by what "torsion" soul
became partly autonomous, waking self. The evolution of
image is found on the walls leading to a separate altar-like
wall where two bison are depicted *about* to couple but are
held in suspension just prior to the act:

> it is that spot where the leap should occur that
> Le Tuc D'Audoubert says is VOID, and that unfilled
> space between two fertile poles here feels like the origin
> of the abyss, as if in the minds of those who shaped and
> placed these two bison, fertilization was pulled free,
> and that freedom from connection is the demon of crea-
> tion haunting man and woman ever since—

It is Eshleman's way of explaining the birth of abstraction, the literal death of things into fixed images, each held
in the suspension of consciousness, in sterile discontinuity
from the other. Thus, the river that suggests to us subjectivity and dreams in romantic poetry is actually the memory
of the cave's own integrity as a realm of continuous imagistic
thought, on whose walls he now finds the birth of the first
real abstraction, a picture of, not the actuality of, copulation.
The poems of part II of *Fracture*, "The Paleolithic

Dimension," are about the loss of Hades and the soul; its frayed terminals spread out as images and painted dots on the walls of the caves, where modern consciousness goes about inspecting the wreckage of mental exile.

> At the end of 15,000 years of image we are
> *gathered* here, more totally than we now suspect,
> by black manganese turds containing
>
> the seeds of narrative, or berries which
> like that bird we must take in mouth and chew,
> or like two other birds perch
>
> on a sausage of excrement emerging from a headless
> reindeer's anus and kiss, or make love
> talk on this tiny writhing hill of our hunger to sound
>
> ourselves while falls, suspended over us,
> the shadow of what we are—
>
> ("The Seeds of Narrative," *F* 57)

Though image has always been the preeminent thing in Eshleman's lyricism, the poetry of *Fracture* has become almost purely imagistic. There is little commentary left in the discourse, where image is seized and decoded, or seized and linked to other images in an argument. The reader will sometimes feel as if there is no longer a mediator here between the deep state of sleep and the conscious world of a text. That mediating function of the poet/narrator, standing between imagination and sense, has shrunk noticeably to the voice of his occasional end notes to poems where he is "objective" in tone, as Eshleman drives his language toward the pole of sleep, the poem as the clustered imagery of irrational awareness and little else. What narrative we perceive is within the image content itself, a kind of inner dream logic that derives its own sequentiality from undifferentiated lodes of memory, fantasy, and association.

Both Eshleman and Hillman assume that the voice of the dreaming intellect, "the imaginal ego (not *my ego*)," as Eshleman points out in the Introduction, is untranslatable into any other language. To adulterate it with commentary or rational deciphering is to ignore its needs, desires, its view of the world from underneath. If we find an "I" in the poetry, it is not the mediating poet's persona but his dreamed self, the opposite of the waking ego. That is the only true opposite of selfhood Hillman *or* Eshleman can hypothesize. Putting this negative ego in the poem is the only solution to how one is to view a "fallen" world of human exile from the vantage point of an underworld's other set of relations. Eshleman thus turns tables on us in these poems—by "reading" *this* world from the dream state of his lyricism.

To read an Eshleman poem properly, one must assume that the text will pull away from us almost from the start of its discourse, or has already done so prior to its beginning on the page. We enter the poem hoping to sift and clarify and reduce imagery to context and theme, to get from imagination into world. But Eshleman's poem will wind back, down, into the sleep state while keeping up a chattering commentary that is increasingly lateral in its imagery, until image-chains simply take over and we are left hearing a dream recount itself from behind the wall of sleep. A set of notes and lyric responses to cave lore, in the poem "A Kind of Moisture on the Wall," begins with this semblance of commentary,

> Suppose earliest consciousness is worked off the shape
> of certain earth inevitabilities, that the shape of Cro-
> Magnon "consciousness" is the contour grid of those
> specific caves he chose to paint and engrave.

But by the next page, we have left behind these mediating words to enter the dreamscape,

A headless shoulderless woman running filled with lances
across the rock of a tautly pinned elk is the sensation
        of imagination
as it pours through life like hoarfrost, or liquid jade,
the rock wall itself writhes so stilly
that something never to be completed writhes in us,
ringworm intrigues, the tentacular lava of maggot-
lined fables. The moment we touch anything
that touches us the entire human body becomes a
        pipeline
of inverse fire hydrants wrenching shut the feeling
        valves,
for to totally connect with even the stain of an image
is fearsome, a cog to cog movement in the interlocking twister of an enrapt reporter calling up
the abandoned elevators of the lower simian body
derailed in Africa millenniums before, those rotting
        luncheonettes
visited only by hyenas and ferocious striped worms,
those bleached cabooses individuation pretends
to have left behind but which lurch open into our
        brains in dream
to keep up open to the future of an earth
awesome, infinite, coiled in hypnosis.

(F 81–82)

Eshleman's imaginal ego is thus on the side of the
caves, and speaks as their advocate—as if he were in fact
the voice of certain of these images that *we* are observing
on the walls. That trope of a voice within an image, speaking from behind the image in the continuum of the underworld, works its way all through the book and into *Hotel
Cro-Magnon*. It is the new locus of voice; if we look for a
stance now, we can only assume that it comes to us much
as Tiresias did to Odysseus, as a lingering kind of language-
consciousness within the confines of sleep and death.
Eshleman has not invented a new persona or a new context

for its identity—we are not far removed from romantic poetics or symbolist lyric, but we do have a new venue, the caves of the Dordogne, which stand for all the archetypal loci of imagination at once: as the cavity of the head itself, the ear, the mouth, the womb and uterus, and as literal cave. Eshleman would also have us extend the archetype to bedroom, nursery, coffin, burial pit, graveyard, and tangentially, even Christian hell. The cave is the totality of darkness, unconsciousness, dreams, and the body's own inner world of wilderness forces.

If we take this imaginal ego into other regions of culture, such as the world of Disney cartoons, we are guided by a sleeping persona whose wisdom comes entirely from his dreams. In the third section of *Fracture,* a poem entitled "The Tomb of Donald Duck," we are not all that far removed from the methodology of *The Waste Land,* where a similar dreaming voice surveys the underworld of post-war London from his perspective as the dead Tiresias. Even Eliot's footnotes work the same manipulation of tones and presumed objectivity that we find in Eshleman, but Eshleman goes farther, and deploys more of the techniques of surrealism to intensify this feeling that we inhabit the speaker's dreaming visions.

The theme of this section is again the loss of the underworld in a civilization that has sealed it off and built its towers of consciousness on its remains. We are at the *tomb* of so-called animations, which are only the soulless representatives of certain fantasies of the conscious mind. Disney's "animals" are thin disguises for anthropocentric awareness. The wall separating upper and lower worlds now turns to glass, a new motif of this section, and the cave wall has become the silver screen of pop culture. What we see projected as image is not from underneath, but from *the other side,* the dayworld of conscious thought; hence, Disney's metaphors point back to the waking ego, selfhood, and not to the great natural underworld. Disney's images are the opposite of cave art, and are a needle "injecting adult anxieties / into [a child's] neoteny" (*F* 93).

In "Toddler Under Glass," Eshleman sees himself as the frozen image brought in like a cooked pheasant for adults to admire. The poem quotes liberally from the actual "Baby Book" his father kept of his first three years; there are photographs marking stages of his infancy, with copious notes recording weight gain, height, first steps, and first words. The persona sees the record kept by his father as a terrifying chronicle of a child stepping away from his freedom in the underworld, losing step by step his access to imagination as he enters the adult world's consciousness. Mouthing his first words is a tragic parturition from Persephone's realm,

> Bok *old* mamma, tak-a *new* mamma
> bit of wa-wa words
> bok windmill sound child, bunched on the social platter
> a baby mammoth in the peekaboo

which prompts the adult persona to remark in closing,

> I see you snow mounting from below.

> (*F* 95)

"In essence we do not want to be outside," begins the next section, "The Severing," a stunning commentary on the death of the underworld and the appearance of such Hillmanian villains as Hercules, the hero as killer, who, along with Disney's animated caricatures of animals, mark the loss of affinity with the natural world. The "satanized underworld" turns the whole of beast imagery into terrifying devils, as even Donald Duck

. . . has the power to leave the duck
as hagfish are said to leave their lairs at dusk
to all night long bore into the souls of children.

(F 98)

In "Manticore Vortex," the fourth and final part of *Fracture*, we tour the sterile landscapes of mere consciousness, the alien life that drifts through its streets and commits its atrocities against the few human cultures that still linger in the shadow of the dream state. This is Eshleman's "Waste Land" sequence, a brilliant working out of the theme of the alienated soul incapable of reaching through to its living counterpart in self. The consequence of such alienation is a loss of reality, an overwhelming fantasy of life devouring what was once an actual world. "We do not know that we are deep in fantasy— / we only know we are frightened," he writes in "Certification," the opening poem. The soul has become a giant fantasm of fearful powers, the paranoid projection of a self that has denied its underside too long. The world has gone mad with fear of the unconscious, as we get this Hans Bellmer dreamscape of contemporary life:

As for me, I only released the white crocodile built
like a good cause in the trap of my heterosexual
        slingshot,
along with a volley of old Plymouth backseats,
each with a coed's head stuffed into its corner,
her spread North American legs seborrheic
though still housed in bobby-sox . . . .
            . . . I could see that Europa
holding on for dear life was the Venus of Laussel
vomiting through her bull-horn the Pleistocene
        conquest.

("Millennium," F 108)

"The Language Orphan" captures the rootless "I" of waking as "what is anonymous at the heart of all / crawl[ing] in place." Only "in dream," can one join this figment of personality, this fiction of language itself, who "keeps drawing home through you." The "other" self who stands unused beside this "I" is the "unused needle" of a compass, and "home," the underworld of dream, is the "infinite thread."

Fracture's title refers to many things—a broken ankle, the fissure that opens up to underworlds in the caves, dreaming; but there is a final way to regard this work and its intentions: the fracture that is exposed between day and night selves, the literal ego of consciousness in its sterile waste land, and the night ego that mocks, derides, grotesquely satirizes the day world's activities. We get both voices in the poetry, a true Bakhtinian dialogism of the two sides of self, and the space between is the deep fracture over which the two voices cannot connect. That is the human tragedy in Eshleman's tale; evolution and the casting out of a psychic paradise into selfhood meant the great divide would open in the mind. Even so, the constant vacillation between the two voices or two realms of experience, sleeping and waking, makes the reader realize that here indeed is a lyric language that is juxtaposing two visions so often, they begin to merge—if not in the poetry then in the reader! It is we who find ourselves in a textual landscape of comparative realities, and who are witness to their maddening distinctions and contrapuntal systems.

Eshleman does precisely what Hillman advises psychotherapy to undertake: the interpretation of the nightworld in terms of the night and dreaming, not in terms of the day. We watch the day's world emerge in scenes of brutal warfare, corrupt imperialism, the fantasia of contemporary social reality, and are drawn to Eshleman's imaginal perspective, whose values subtly become our own. We are made to withdraw from this day world as it is, to reject its fantasm and to expect to find it exploding under the gaze of this other persona, the dreamer's voice.

To the degree we do so, at Eshleman's insistence, we have moved out of the sphere of our own esthetics and into that of South America, Spain, the dark world of Artaud, Soutine, Francis Bacon—the web of esthetic relations drawn up as Eshleman's own personal tradition. The price he has paid in his poetry for this other heritage is a loss of clarity, of stark, even blunt arguments, the beauties of abstraction that are the hallmark of the Protestant esthetic tradition. In siding with forces outside English, Eshleman has plunged himself deep in a contrary mode of thought—call it the "Catholic" imagination, with its deep faith in the powers of image to transubtantiate matter into spirit. Eshleman *uses* that lode of image and mystery without converting to its faith, and thus has no constant quarrel with the church and its brutal history of repression; his poetry appropriates the very sources of image Pound sought in Italian Renaissance and French Troubadour poetry, but both were white Americans of Protestant descent who remained outsiders in their pursuit of an alternative tradition. Both refused to accept the theological roots of the esthetic they grafted to their imaginations; but each pushed American poetry closer to the pole of dreams and the fluid world of pagan imagism as a result of their efforts.

And because neither Pound nor Eshleman could accept the *faith* behind the image, but chose instead some earlier root of pre-Christian belief as a *possible* theology, they avoided the trap of religious idealism that has seized so many other poets; they had no faith with which to proselytize their readers. Eshleman has remained the visionary of no easy solutions; he has shunned the ecological idealists of his time, and turned his back on other grand schemes of reformation for the age. He has remained the satirist, the mocking voice of underworld laughter, and reserved for his prose his assaults on the naive ideologies his contemporaries have resorted to for answers. Indeed, this is the real force of *Antiphonal Swing,* with its bristling defense of Bakhtinian derision as the great power of certain 20th century artists—whose work sides with no ideological camp but instead concentrates on stripping each datum of waking into its nightsoul, if it has one.

It is within this insistent imaginal perspective that experience is rendered, drawn in. And I think it is just here that we discover the achievement of Eshleman's poetry—he has made us the imaginal eyes on life, and as readers we are no longer looking at the dreamer apart from ourselves, but have been given Pan's mind in which to think, observe, react to the modern world. Pan is the figure who has come back to life in Eshleman's lyrical exuberance and hyperbole; only Pan belongs to a world that favors the nightside and who jeers at the workings of mere consciousness in human beings. Pan is the child of Hermes, the product of a seduction between the underworld's messenger and a shepherdess, or, as I suspect may be the real intent of the myth of his genesis, the product of Hermes' seduction of a goat. His hooved feet and capering sexual nature make him the half-man, half-goat who joins lower and upper worlds, and who is, like his father, another messenger, but in this life, the day's world—where he traffics steadily in the realms of mind and genital, body wisdom. Pan, who is the best embodiment for the lyric persona Eshleman has consolidated in these later books on cave lore and underworlds, is the figure in whom the phallus is once more a unifying and expressive force of a wholeness of human nature. Pan's love arises from his knowledge of death, which he celebrates in his exuberant disrespect for mere literal being.

It is as Pan then that Eshleman imagines the world, and because we are party to his lyric enterprise, we must share the mind of Pan with him when we inspect contemporary culture and experience. We are given pagan pantheism as a religion, and our view of material life is suddenly charged with animist visions, a vista on nature that acknowledges its own soul and imagination, its own creative will. The glorification of nature is, in fact, the essence of Pound's tradition and the lineage from which Eshleman draws his poetics as a writer.

We are given the pure instance of that pantheistic vision, through the eyes of his Pan-persona, in the opening poem of *Hotel Cro-Magnon*, "Apotheosis," which insists that

> One need go no further for satisfaction with the earth.
> "Nature is imagination itself"
>
> The surf lace flows   blowsy oyster frill
> anal flavors   uroboric orals
>
> seamless,   the day is sloth and ray
>   moving under the language film
>   as breasts, or turtles
>
> and so, breaking through enthusiasm

Nature is language breaking through to the mind, the very gist of Pound's vision, for such language is *enthousiasmos*, ensouled, or as Eshleman defines it, "possessed by the god,"

> the beautiful chains of surf which reaching
>   the apex of their heave
>   recross this tawny rose to reveal
>   the saddle of Persephone flecked by Zeus
>
> (*HCM* 17)

The darkly humorous tirades against the world in "Reagan at Bitberg," "Variations on Jesus and the Fly," "Children of the Monosyllable," and other poems of *Hotel Cro-Magnon,* are Bakhtin's "carnival laughter," Pan's mordant guffaw over the waking world. In "Pan's Signal Tower," based on a painting by David True, we hear of the "fructifying abyss" where "the power of the / womb / crosses the power of the tomb," death and birth joining to form what in another poem he refers to as a "twomb," the completed conception of the underworld as both sex and death at once, where the airborne Pan flies over "the Grand Canyon of the mind" (*HCM* 116). "There is no wall between my dying and my face before birth," he tells us in "At the Cleveland Museum of Art" (*HCM* 73), where the infinite underworld surrounds the ego in its narrow life.

Indeed, the "House of Eshleman" which he has been destroying by means of his lyric raids on the dream-self, is fast becoming a foundation for a new house, at first "Pan's signal tower," but soon enough we are aware that the new house is in essence the great historic continuum of imagination he calls the Hotel Cro-Magnon. Here is an actual hotel built a few yards away from the *abri* or shelter of Cro-Magnon man, " 'Cro-Magnon' meaning 'big hole' in the local patois" (Prologue, *HCM* 9), where the contemporary guest lies down in the dark with the great dead and dreams their collective dream:

> We ourselves are the same as Cro-Magnon, no matter the plethora of interfaces between us and nature. . . . Poetry twists toward the unknown and seeks to realize something beyond the poet's initial awareness. What it seeks to know might be described as the unlimited interiority of its initial impetus.

With the construction of Pan as his persona and a house made of the sheltering roofs of the Hotel Cro-Magnon, Eshleman completes the cycle of his autobiography; he has moved into a mythological space he can sincerely claim as home. The sense of moving in, settling anew, sinking roots shapes the theme of the poems in section 3; and we may take from these poems, "Moving," "Looking for a House," and "Looking Up Through the Christmas Tree at 51," which opens suggestively enough, "So I'm buried here, happily buried, / at the base" (*HCM* 80), that he has reached an end to running away from Indiana and the first house. The self will never entirely stop wandering, however; the dream is ever an initiation into death, or, as these poems argue, each act of imagination is a voyage into death and the sexual self, a descent toward the soul.

There is for the first time in his poetry the certainty of possessing imagination in this grander sense of a mythic intelligence, and of having conceived a persona in whom to invest poetic faith. The pagan vision emerging from these later poems coincides with the larger turning toward animist, pagan imagination in the mature work of his original circle. Diane Wakoski's poetry has also veered steadily toward a vision of the underworld and its principal heroines, Persephone, Medea, and Eurydice; Robert Kelly's poetry is a lush jungle of animist visions and of the female as deity of nature and imagination. Armand Schwerner's *Tablets* recreate the paleolithic intelligence as it inscribed its preliminary consciousness onto clay, replete with hieroglyphs, lacunae, and stammerings into dreams. Jerome Rothenberg's "ethnopoetic" canon has evolved a vision of elemental heroes, among them "Cok Boy," the phallic Pan whose voyages take him to other parts of the wasteland of contemporary consciousness and its dread of death and total love. Rochelle Owens' recastings of Old Testament cosmogony are from a pagan perspective, with the female intelligence at its center and a delight in the wholeness of human nature that is essentially pagan.

Eshleman's writing illuminates a tendency shared by numerous writers and artists of the second half of the century. His search for psychological alternatives, for a way out of mere "life emptied of its primal scene," which led him to conceive of the underworld as unconsciousness, as the depths of the body and of collective nature, joins his work to a much larger force within experimental writing in this era—as Western confidence in its own reality has broken down and allowed the experimental artist to revive certain dreaded heresies of pagan thought, the creative function of death, the world as ensouled, and the wisdom of the dream. Eshleman's peculiar *minding* of that underworld of self, "the vault of cosmic womb mates," is his unique poetic achievement within a vast context of supporting texts. What we mean by postmodernism, late and fading as it may be, is ultimately this view of the world beyond the borders of Western Christian understanding.

NOTES

On pages: Text:

10 F. O. Matthiessen, *American Renaissance: Art and Expression in the Age of Emerson and Whitman* (New York: Oxford University Press, 1941, 1968).

12 Jerome and Diane Rothenberg, eds. *Symposium of the Whole: A Range of Discourse Toward an Ethnopoetics* (Berkeley: University of California Press, 1983).

17 Octavio Paz, *The Bow and the Lyre* (Austin, TX: University of Texas Press, 1973).

18 Charles Olson, "Fable for Slumber," ed. George F. Butterick, *Sulfur* 12: 1986.

27 Gary Snyder, "The Politics of Ethnopoetics," in *The Old Ways: Six Essays* (San Francisco: City Lights Books, 1977), pp. 15–43; also contains the essay, "The Incredible Survival of Coyote," rpt. in part in *Symposium,* pp. 425–33.

Charles Olson, *Call Me Ishmael* (New York: Reynal & Hitchcock, 1947; rpt. New York: Grove Press, 1958; and San Francisco: City Lights Books, 1971).

33 Charles Olson, "The Kingfishers," in *The Collected Poems of Charles Olson,* ed. George F. Butterick (Berkeley: University of California Press, 1987), pp. 86–93.

The New American Poetry: 1945–1960 (New York: Grove Press, 1960).

Eric Berne, *The Structure and Dynamics of Organizations and Groups* (New York: Ballantine Books, 1963). See also Eric Berne, *Group Treatment* (New York: Grove Press, 1967) and Michael S. Olmsted, *The Small Group* (New York: Random House, 1959).

36 *Statement* (Los Angeles: Black Sparrow Press, 1968). *Statement* is a pamphlet announcing the publication of books by various figures from the "deep image" group. The cover lists Antin, Economou, Eshleman, Mac Low, Owens, Rothenberg, Schwerner and Wakoski.

   On the break-up of the group, Rothenberg commented in 1984, "Well, I've a mixed sense of it over the years: there was that early personal relationship with [Kelly], more than with the other poets that you mentioned, but we drifted apart later and never really have got back to it. . . . People like Schwerner and Eshleman and Mac Low remain perennially close—not only ideas but poetics/approaches to writing." *The Riverside Interview* 4, ed. Gavin Selerie and Eric Mottram (London: Binnacle Press, 1984).

37 Conversations with Diane Wakoski at the Chicago MLA Convention, December 28–29, 1990.

   For further discussion of "deep image" poetics see Robert Kelly, "Notes on Deep Image," *Trobar* 2: 1961; Rothenberg, "Why Deep Image?" *Trobar* 3: 1961; "The Deep Image Is the Threatened Image," *Poems for the Floating World* 4: 1962; and (with Robert Creeley), "An Exchange: Deep Image & Mode," *Kulchur* 6: 1962. Selections from the "Exchange" were reprinted in Rothenberg's selected prose, *Pre-Faces and Other Writings* (New York: New Directions, 1981). The role of Robert Bly, James Wright, W. S. Merwin, poetry editor of *The Nation* 1960–1961, and others had in formulating other approaches to the "deep image" falls outside the scope of this book.

38 Jerome Rothenberg, ed. *Ritual* (New York: Something Else Press, 1966); *Technicians of the Sacred* (Berkeley: University of California Press, 1968; rev. ed. 1985).

41 Jerome Rothenberg, ed. *Shaking the Pumpkin: Traditional Poetry of the Indian North Americans* (New York: Alfred van der Marck Editions, 1971; rev. ed. 1986).

45 Pablo Neruda, *Residence on Earth,* trans. Clayton Eshleman (San Francisco: Amber House Press, 1962).

48 Clayton Eshleman, review of William Bronk, *Life Supports: New and Collected Poems* (San Francisco: North Point Press, 1981), in *Los Angeles Times Sunday Book Review:* November 15, 1981; rpt. *Antiphonal Swing: Selected Prose 1962 / 1987,* pp. 76–79; review of Elizabeth Bishop, *The Complete Poems: 1927–1979* (New York: Farrar, Straus, Giroux, 1983) in *Los Angeles Times Sunday Book Review:* April 17, 1983; rpt. in *Antiphonal Swing,* pp. 71–75.

49 Clayton Eshleman, *Novices: A Study of Poetic Apprenticeship* (Los Angeles: Mercer and Aitchison, 1989), p. 24.

51 Clayton Eshleman, *On Mules Sent from Chavin* (Swansea, U.K.: Galloping Dog Press, 1977).

Charles Olson, *Mayan Letters*, ed. Robert Creeley (Mallorca: Divers Press, 1953; rpt. London: Cape, 1968); Allen Ginsberg, *Journals: Early Fifties Early Sixties*, ed. Gordon Hall (New York: Grove Press, 1977).

53 Clayton Eshleman, "The Book of Yorunomado" appeared in its original form in *Indiana*; revised as "Webs of Entry" in *Coils*; a 1964 version was used in *The Name Encanyoned River*, pp. 21–27.

56 Robert Creeley, *Words* (New York: Charles Scribner's Sons, 1967); *Pieces* (New York: Charles Scribner's Sons, 1969).

61 Mikhail Bakhtin, *Rabelais and His World*, trans. Helene Iswolsky (Cambridge, MA: M.I.T. Press, 1968).

63 James Hillman, *The Dream and the Underworld* (New York: Harper & Row, 1979).

65 Clayton Eshleman, *Antonin Artaud: 4 Texts* (Los Angeles: Panjandrum Books, 1982); *Core Meander* (Santa Barbara, CA: Black Sparrow Press, 1977); *Grotesca* (London: New London Pride, 1977).

70 Clayton Eshleman, "Response to Mary Kinzie," *Sulfur* 13 (Spring 1985): 153–57; rpt. in *Antiphonal Swing*, pp. 199–204.

71 August Kleinzhaler, *Earthquake Weather* (Mt. Kisco, NY: Moyer Bell Ltd., 1989).

72 Charles Olson, "Projective Verse," *Selected Writings of Charles Olson*, ed. Robert Creeley (New York: New Directions, 1966).

Alfred North Whitehead, *Process and Reality: An Essay in Cosmology* (New York: Harper Torchbooks, 1960).

79 J. D. Salinger, *Catcher in the Rye* (Boston: Little, Brown, 1951); Jack Kerouac, *The Town & the City* (New York: Harcourt, Brace, 1950); John Clellon Holmes, *Go* (New York: Scribner's, 1952); Jack Kerouac, *On the Road* (New York: Viking, 1957).

83 According to Eshleman, Kelly's treatment of the book went beyond critical indifference and broke "a publishing commitment to the book," which he then reduced to a distributing agreement, on which he also reneged. Two hundred copies of the book were sent to Kelly for distribution, but correspondence broke off, and the books were stored in unopened cartons in Kelly's basement for six years. According to Eshleman, Kelly "deserved to be rebuked . . . for insincerity + irresponsibility." From a note by Eshleman in response to my version of events.

90 César Vallejo, *Poemas humanos: Human Poems*, trans. Clayton
Eshleman (New York: Grove Press, 1968).

"All in all, I have spent over 16 years on Vallejo, and the
1979 edition of the posthumous poetry is based on an 18th draft
of 112 poems. It is impossible here to even suggest how I man-
aged to learn from each of those drafts. Going over the same poems
again and again made me aware of the slipperyness as well as the
rocklike quality of languages and of the space between two
languages, in a way that reading a text in English, even several
times, never does. For me, Vallejo was the great test of apprenticeship. At times, it was mainly a matter of how to stay with it
when again and again I could not get the Spanish text to yield
a precise meaning, that I could be sure of, that I could shape into
something that seemed accurate to it in English.

"Apprenticeship, in all its shapes, should test the endurance
of the novice, it should be the roughest mountain he knows to
climb and should show, in the way he handles it, his ability to
not only absorb but to assimilate influence.

"And does one really ever end apprenticeship? The great
dead never cease to talk to the poet and perhaps one way to suggest the point at which apprenticeship is no longer felt as such
is when the masters become allies instead of oppositions."

from *A Note on Apprenticeship* (Chicago: Two Hands
Press, 1979).

91 Clayton Eshleman, *The House of Okumura* (Toronto: Weed/Flower
Press, 1969).

92 Carl Gustaf Jung, *Symbols of Transformation: An Analysis of the
Prelude to a Case of Schizophrenia*, trans. R. F. C. Hull, 2nd ed.
(Princeton: Princeton University Press, 1967).

Erich Neumann, *The Origins and History of Consciousness*, trans.
R. F. C. Hull, Bollingen Series XLII (Princeton: Princeton University Press, 1954, 1973).

98 Jonathan Katz, ed. *Gay American History: Lesbians and Gay Men
in the U.S.A.* (New York: Thomas Y. Crowell, 1976).

Martin Duberman, *Black Mountain: An Exploration in Community* (New York: Anchor Books, 1973).

101 Clayton Eshleman, *Walks, Caterpillar* X (1967).

Robert Duncan, *Roots and Branches* (New York: New Directions,
1964); *Bending the Bow* (New York: New Directions, 1968).

105 D. H. Lawrence, *St. Mawr and The Man Who Died* (New York:
Vintage Books, n.d.), p. 202. Lawrence's Christ/Quetzalcoatl/Osiris
figure is the essential model of the "restored man" for Olson as
well as for Eshleman.

110 "What our fathers are, as poets, is a tangled bank of visionary poetic fathers, masters in the traditional sense, as well as the flesh and blood father, of constraints in the creative process. The thought that one gets free makes less sense than the thought that one frees oneself by participation within a sense of speech that one has made one's own."

from A Note on Apprenticeship

The phrase "the tangled bank" comes from Stanley Edgar Hyman's *The Tangled Bank: Darwin, Marx, Freud and Frazer as Imaginative Writers* (New York: Atheneum, 1962). Hyman remarks that his phrase comes from Shakespeare, but standard concordances do not list it in any of the dramatic or lyric works.

112 Charles Olson, *The Special View of History,* ed. Ann Charters (Berkeley: Oyez, 1970).

117 For a possible source of "Diagonal," cf. Paul Blackburn's poem "The Slogan," written 1965/67, in *The Collected Poems of Paul Blackburn,* ed. Edith Jarolim (New York: Persea Books, 1985), pp. 359–60.

118 Eshleman informs me that my point about self-cleansing in this poem is "totally wrong"; "my intention," he writes in a note, "was to show the laundry as a slave-labor shop that I was able to *see* (= perceive) via work on my own life." Rereading the poem from this viewpoint ties together certain images, but the reading is too literal: given the poem's place in the closing section of *Indiana,* I am convinced the deeper intention is to dramatize a rebirth in the baptismal setting of a laundry, a fresh use of the meaning of cleansing and of new clothes.

122 Charles Olson, *The Maximus Poems* (New York: Jargon/Corinth Books, 1960), p. 4.

123 Jerome Rothenberg, *New Selected Poems* (New York: New Directions, 1986), pp. 69–73.

125 Paul Goodman, *Growing Up Absurd: Problems of Youth in Organized Society* (New York: Vintage Books, 1960).

129 Allen Ginsberg, "The Green Automobile," *Collected Poems: 1947–1980* (New York: Harper & Row, 1984), pp. 83–87; first published in *Reality Sandwiches* (San Francisco: City Lights Books, 1963).

130 Wilhelm Reich, *The Mass Psychology of Fascism,* trans. Vincent R. Carfagno (New York: Farrar, Straus, Giroux, 1974).

132–33 David W. Wainhouse, *Remnants of Empire: The United States and the End of Colonialism* (New York: Harper & Row, 1964).

136 Allen Ginsberg, *Howl and Other Poems* (San Francisco: City Lights Books, 1956).

137 Serge Guilbaut, *How New York Stole the Idea of Modern Art: Abstract Expressionism, Freedom, and the Cold War* (Chicago: University of Chicago Press, 1983).

142 Robert Duncan, *The Opening of the Field* (New York: New Directions, 1960).

146 Charles Olson, *Proprioception* (San Francisco: Four Seasons Foundation, 1965); rpt. in *Additional Prose,* ed. George F. Butterick (Bolinas, CA: Four Seasons Foundation, 1974), pp. 17–35.

147 See T. S. Eliot's "The Three Voices of Poetry," in *On Poetry and Poets* (New York: Farrar, Straus, & Giroux, 1957), pp. 106–09, and C. K. Stead's chapter, "Eliot's "Dark Embryo' " in *The New Poetic: Yeats to Eliot* (New York: Harper Torchbooks, 1964), pp. 125–47.

T. S. Eliot, *Four Quartets* (New York: Harcourt, Brace, 1943; London: Faber and Faber, 1959).

148 Clayton Eshleman, "The Stevens-Artaud Rainbow," *Margins* [London]: 1988; rpt. in *Antiphonal Swing,* pp. 245–53.

151 Sam Shepard, *The Unseen Hand and Other Plays* (New York: Bantam Books, 1986).

153 Gustave Flaubert, *The Temptation of St. Anthony,* trans. Kitty Mrossovsky (Ithaca, NY: Cornell University Press, 1981).

Charles Olson, *In Cold Hell, In Thicket* (Mallorca: The Divers Press, 1953); rpt. in *Archaeologist of Morning,* and in *The Collected Poems;* Denise Levertov, *With Eyes at the Back of Our Heads* (New York: New Directions, 1959); Robert Duncan, *The Opening of the Field* (New York: New Directions, 1960).

163 César Vallejo, *The Complete Posthumous Poetry,* trans. Clayton Eshleman and José Rubia Barcia (Berkeley: University of California Press, 1978).

165 Diane Wakoski, *Smudging* (Los Angeles: Black Sparrow Press, 1972).

180 Sigmund Freud, *The Interpretation of Dreams,* trans. A. A. Brill (New York: Random House, 1950).

183 George C. Herring, *America's Longest War: The United States and Viet-Nam, 1950–1975* (New York: John Wiley & Sons, 1979).

185 Mircea Eliade, *The Myth of the Eternal Return* (New York: Bollingen/Pantheon Books, 1959).

Though portions of "Heaven-Bands" have been published in various journals, the whole has not appeared in book form.

188 John McLaughlin, "Interview with Clayton Eshleman," *Southern California Anthology* (1985).

190 César Vallejo, *Spain, Take This Cup from Me,* trans. Clayton Eshleman and José Rubia Barcia (New York: Grove Press, 1974); Antonin Artaud, *Letter to André Breton,* trans. Clayton Eshleman, *Sparrow* 23 (1974); Artaud, *To Have Done with the Judgment of God,* trans. Clayton Eshleman (Los Angeles: Black Sparrow Press, 1975), and Vallejo, *Battles in Spain: Five Unpublished Poems,* trans. Clayton Eshleman (Santa Barbara, CA: Black Sparrow Press, 1978).

192 Norman O. Brown, *Life Against Death: The Psychoanalytic Meaning of History* (New York: Vintage, 1959).

194 Armand Schwerner, *sounds of the river naranjana and The Tablets I–XXVI* (New York: Station Hill, 1983).

200 Roger Shattuck, *The Banquet Years: The Origins of the Avant Garde in France 1885 to World War I,* rev. ed. (New York: Vintage Books, 1968), pp. 329, 331.

209 "A Jewish giant at home with his parents in the Bronx, N.Y. 1970,'' *Diane Arbus* (New York: Aperture, 1972), p. [57].

225–26 Among those supporting texts are Kelly's *The Book of Persephone* (New York: Treacle Press, 1978); *Flesh Dream Book* (Los Angeles: Black Sparrow Press, 1971); *The Flowers of Unceasing Coincidence* (Barrytown, NY: Station Hill, 1988); Rochelle Owens' *The Joe 82 Creation Poems* (Los Angeles: Black Sparrow Press, 1974) and *The Joe Chronicles, part 2* (Santa Barbara, CA: Black Sparrow Press, 1979); Jerome Rothenberg's *New Selected Poems* and *Khûrbn and Other Poems* (New York: New Directions, 1989); Wakoski's *Emerald Ice: Selected Poems 1962–1987* (Santa Rosa, CA: Black Sparrow Press, 1988), and *Medea the Sorceress* (Santa Rosa, CA: Black Sparrow Press, 1991).

Index

Adler, Alfred, 202, 209
Allen, Donald M., 82
    The New American Poetry, 33, 44, 76
    The Poetics of the New American Poetry, 44
American midwest, 21–21, 125
Amin, Idi, 170
Antin, David, 10, 33, 37, 115, 228n
Arbus, Diane, 209, 233n
Ark, The, 82
Artaud, Antonin, 19, 31, 57, 59, 64, 65, 75, 108, 191, 221, 229n, 233n
    Letter to André Breton, 190
    To Have Done with the Judgment of God, 190
Ashbery, John, 70, 71

Bacon, Francis, 58, 221
Bakhtin, Mikhail, 61, 62, 69, 74, 169, 191, 192, 194, 220, 222, 229n
    Rabelais and His World, 61–62, 190
Barcia, José Rubia, 190
Barth, John, 147
Barthes, Roland, 44
Beckett, Samuel,
    Endgame, 151
    Happy Days, 151, 155
    Krapp's Last Tape, 151
    Waiting for Godot, 151
Bellmer, Hans, 219
Berne, Eric,
    The Structure and Dynamics of Organizations and Groups, 33, 228n
Bernstein, Charles, 149

Big Table, 82
Bishop, Elizabeth, 48, 228n
Black Mountain Review, 45, 82
Blackburn, Paul, 51, 57, 69, 75, 103, 120, 121, 185, 203, 206, 231n
Blake, William, 12, 19, 32, 52, 69, 71, 83, 90, 106, 107, 108, 117, 120, 141, 172
    "The Marriage of Heaven and Hell," 59, 105
    "The Mental Traveler," 172
Bly, Robert, 37, 188, 228n
Bloom, Harold, 74
Borges, Jorge Luis, 88
Bosch, Hieronymous, 189
Brando, Marlon, 79
Breton, André, 137
Bronk, William, 48, 228n
    Life Supports, 48
    The New World, 48
Brown, Norman O., 169, 192, 193, 204, 223n
    Life Against Death, 192–93
Buber, Martin, 12
Burroughs, William, 51
Butterick, George F., 227n

Cage, John, 37
Calvo, César, 97, 99, 100, 110
Cavalcanti, Guido, 50
Caron, Leslie, 129
Cassady, Neal, 79, 80
Castañeda, Carlos, 171
Celan, Paul, 75
Césaire, Aimée, 31, 75, 190
    "On Negritude," 41
Cézanne, Paul, 179
Chelsea Review, 82
City Lights, 82
"Communist Manifesto," 41
Conrad, Joseph, 60, 147, 148
Corman, Cid, 47, 75, 83, 186
Corso, Gregory, 37, 45, 79
    "The Mad Yak," 37
Cousteau, Jacques, 143
Crane, Hart, 103, 119, 206
Creeley, Robert, 45, 51, 56, 75, 82, 228n, 229
    Pieces, 56
    Words, 56
Cumont, Franz
    After Life in Roman Paganism, 198

Dahlberg, Edward, 9
Dante, 177, 206, 207, 211
Darwin, Charles, 178, 179
Dean, James, 79
Deguy, Michel, 75
deKooning, Willem, 142
Depth psychology, 35–36, 58–59, 91–94, 105, 130–32, 151, 169–70,
    191–93, 196–99, 202, 210–11, 220–21
"Deep Image," 10, 33–38, 115, 225–26
Diamond, Stanley, 26, 44
Disney, Walt, 217, 218
Divus, Andreas, 177
Dreiser, Theodore, 20, 23
Duberman, Martin,
        Black Mountain, 98, 230n
Duncan, Robert, 12, 25, 42, 45, 51, 75, 96, 101, 103, 108, 142, 153,
    230n, 232n
        "An Owl Is an Only Bird of Poetry," 142
        "The Dance," 142
        The Opening of the Field, 153, 232n
        "Passages," 101
        "Rites of Participation," 25
        "Structure of Rime," 101

Economou, George, 33, 34, 35, 228n
Eienhower, Dwight D., 128
Eliade, Mircea, 185, 233n
Eliot, T. S., 147, 177, 182, 217, 232n
        Four Quartets, 147
        "The Love Song of J. Alfred Prufrock," 204
        The Waste Land, 177–78, 180, 217
Emerson, Ralph Waldo, 10, 20
Enslin, Theodore,
        "Synthesis, Part III," 55
Eshleman, Clayton,
        youth: 19, 20, 45–46, 52–54, 83–91, 103, 104, 106, 107–09,
            115–17, 121–22, 125, 138–40, 153–56, 161–62, 172–73,
            218
        marriages: 92, 97, 109, 158–60, 165–66
        maturity: 163–64, 171, 175–76
        poetics: 27–32, 46–50, 75–76, 99–100, 109–10, 118–19,
            209–10, 214–17, 222–23, 225–26
        Altars, 76, 138–41
                "The Dissolution," 139
                "The Gates of Capricorn," 139
                "Lustral Waters," 139
                "The Meadow," 139

Clayton Eshleman (*cont.*)
    Altars (*cont.*)
        "Ode to Reich," 139, 140
        "The Tourbillions," 139
    Antonin Artaud: 4 Texts, 65
    Antiphonal Swing, 222
        "Stevens-Artaud Rainbow," 149–51
    Caterpillar, 11, 54, 55, 57, 101
    Coils, 52, 91, 104, 107, 146–47, 171, 172
        "T'ai," 143
        "The House of Okumura," 151
        "Coils," 131, 140–41
        "The Physical Traveler," 186
        "Trenches," 189
        "Webs of Entry," 94
    Core Meander, 65
    Folio, 45, 46
    Fracture, 9, 23, 53, 63, 198, 200, 207–23
        "Certification," 219
        "The Death of Bill Evans," 209–10
        "A Kind of Moisture on the Wall," 215–16
        "The Language Orphan," 220
        "The Loaded Sleeve of Hades," 211–12
        "Maithuna," 202
        "Manticore Vortex," 67, 73
        "Millennium," 219
        "Notes on a Visit to Le Tuc D'Audoubert," 213
        "Rhapsody," 212
        "The Seeds of Narrative," 214
        "The Severing," 218–19
        "Toddler Under Glass," 218
        "The Tomb of Donald Duck," 217
        "Visions of the Fathers of Lascaux," 67–69, 93, 157, 158, 195, 211
    Grotesca, 65
    The Gull Wall, 57, 58, 171, 192
        "The Gull Wall," 203
        "Portrait of Francis Bacon," 58–59
        "The Ronin Cock," 141, 145–46
        "Study for a Self-Portrait at 12 Years Old," 173
        "To the Creative Spirit," 140
    "Heaven-Bands," 184–85, 186, 187
    Hades in Manganese, 9, 63, 65, 195–206
        "At the Speed of Wine," 206
        "The Aurignacians Have the Floor," 66–67
        "Cimmeria," 203
        "The Decanting," 29–30

Clayton Eshleman (*cont.*)
    Hades in Manganese (*cont.*)
        "Frida Kahlo's Release," 201–02
        "Hades in Manganese," 65–66, 204–06
        "Lich Gate," 65, 195–96, 203, 204
        "A Muscular Man with Gossamer Ways," 199
        "The Shaft," 203
        "Winding Windows," 66
    Hotel Cro-Magnon, 216
        "Apotheosis," 157, 223
        "At the Cleveland Art Museum," 224
        "Children of the Monosyllable," 224
        "Looking for a House," 225
        "Looking Up Through a Christmas Tree at 51," 225
        "Moving," 225
        "A Note and a Fantasia on Ullikummi," 156–57, 158
        "Pan's Signal Tower," 224
        "Reagan at Bitberg," 224
        "Variations on Jesus and the Fly," 224
    The House of Okumura, 91, 151
    Indiana, 47, 52, 88–125, 138, 141, 153, 185
        "The Bank," 109, 114, 115
        "Bear Field," 116
        "The Bedford Vision," 117
        "The Black Hat," 118
        "The 1802 Blake to Butts Letter Variation," 106–07, 110–11
        "The Book of Yorunomado," 47, 53, 89–91, 92, 94, 140
        "Bud Powell," 101, 102–104, 105
        "The Creek," 114, 116
        "The Crocus Bud," 153
        "Diagonal," 117
        "Letter to César Calvo," 97, 99, 100–01, 102, 110
        "The Library," 95
        "Nestual Investigations," 95
        "New Guinea," 114
        "Soutine," 119, 123–25
        "Sunday Afternoon," 120–22
        "Theseus Ariadne," 104, 105
        "The White Tiger," 47, 96
        "The Yellow Garment," 109
    Mexico & North, 45, 82–87, 89, 125
        "La Mujer," 86–87
        "Prothalamion," 87
        "Son of Lightning," 87
        "Water Song," 84–85

Clayton Eshleman (*cont.*)

    The Name Encanyoned River, 152–58, 171–76

        "The Bridge Over the Mayan Pass," 154, 155–56, 158, 172

        "Creation," 174

        "Deeds Done and Suffered by Light," 155

        "Evocation I," 152, 153, 155

    Novices: A Study in Poetic Apprenticeship, 49

    On Mules Sent from Chavin, 51, 52–53

    "Response to Mary Kinzie," 71, 74–75

    Review of *Life Supports*, 48

    "Roaches," 46

    Sulfur, 11

    "Under World Arrest," 31–32

    Walks, 101

    What She Means, 158–71, 174–75, 197

        "Alleluia Choruses," 158

        "August Senex," 175

        "A Climacteric," 175

        "The Cogollo," 168

        "The Dragon Rat Tail," 163–64

        "For Milena Vodickova," 168–69

        "Joseph," 170

        "A Late Evening in July," 175

        "The Name Encanyoned River," 163, 168

        "The Rancid Moonlight Hotel," 127, 171

        "Satanas," 127

        "Still-Life, with African Violets," 169

        "Still-Life, with Fraternity," 162

        "Still-Life, with Manson," 163–64

        "Variations Done for John Digby," 77

Ethnopoetics, 38–44

Eurydice, 204, 225

Evergreen Review, 82

Faulkner, William, 181

    As I Lay Dying, 147

Ferlinghetti, Lawrence, 79

Ferenczi, Sandor, 74

Finnegan, Ruth, 44

Fitzgerald, F. Scott, 22

    The Great Gatsby, 22–23

Flaubert, Gustave,

    The Temptation of Saint Anthony, 153, 232n

Freud, Sigmund, 198
>*The Interpretation of Dreams,* 180, 232n
Fry, Roger, 179

Garcia Lorca, Federico, 49
Gauguin, Paul, 179
"G.I. Bill, The" 77–78
Ginsberg, Allen, 45, 46, 51, 55, 79, 81, 129, 136, 168, 184, 229n,
>231n, 232n
>>"The Green Auto," 129
>>*Howl,* 136, 168
>>*Journals,* 51, 229n
Goethe, Johann Wolfgang von,
>*Faust,* 59
Golub, Leon, 58
Goodman, Paul,
>*Growing Up Absurd,* 125, 231n
Gottlieb, Adolph, 137
Guevara, Che, 111, 112, 119
Goya, Francisco José de, 59, 71
Guilbaut, Serge, 137,
>*How New York Stole the Idea of Modern Art,* 137–38, 232n

Handleman, Sidney, 54, 105, 115, 116
Hawthorne, Nathaniel, 10
Hemingway, Ernest, 181
Hepburn, Audrey, 129
Hercules, 12, 218
Hermes, 222
Herrera, Larco, 101
Herring, George,
>*America's Longest War,* 183–84, 232n
Heyerdahl, Thor, 143
Hillman, James, 63, 64, 69, 74, 85, 175, 177, 191, 192, 193, 194, 196,
>197, 201, 202, 204, 206, 207, 210, 212, 215, 220
>>*The Dream and the Underworld,* 63–64, 177, 191–92, 192–94,
>>>197–98, 229n
>>*Healing Fiction,* 202
Hirschman, Jack, 34, 45
Hitler, Adolf, 170, 171
Ho Chi Minh, 183, 184
Holan, Vladimir, 75
Holmes, John Clellon,
>*Go,* 79, 229n
Homer, 179, 180

Howells, William Dean, 20
Hutton, James, 178
Hyman, Stanley Edgar, 231n

I Ching, 140
Imperialism, 10–11, 12, 21–27, 41, 60, 70, 132–35, 182–84, 203–04
Irby, Ken, 186

Jeffers, Robinson, 182
Joyce, James, 147, 177
    A Portrait of the Artist as a Young Man, 153
    Ulysses, 177, 180
Jung, Carl Gustav, 98, 105, 161
    Symbols of Transformation, 92, 230n

Kahlo, Frida, 201, 202
Katz, Jonathan,
    Gay American History, 98, 230n
Kelly, Robert, 10, 28, 33, 34, 35, 36, 37, 38, 46, 55, 75, 82, 83, 115,
    137, 185, 225, 228n, 229n, 233n
    "Fire Famine," 55
    Sightings and Lunes, 38
    Statement, 36, 227n
Kennedy, John F., 128
Kerouac, Jack, 51, 55, 81, 229n
    On the Road, 79
    The Town and the City, 79
Kesey, Ken, 55
Kinsey, Alfred C., 101
Kinzie, Mary, 71, 74, 229n
    "The Rhapsodic Fallacy," 70
Kleinzhaler, August,
    Earthquake Weather, 71, 229n
Kodalanyi, Gyula, 13
Kulchur, 45

Lawrence, D. H., 108, 131, 231n
    The Man Who Died, 105
    Women in Love, 131–32
Levertov, Denise,
    With Eyes at the Back of Our Heads, 153, 232n
Lewis, P. Wyndham, 180
Lyell, Charles, 178

Mac Low, Jackson, 37, 228n
Malinowski, Bronislaw, 44
Manson, Charles, 162, 163, 164, 170
Mao Tse Tung, 149
Marshall, George C., 183
Marxism, 187, 188
Matthiessen, F. O.,
        American Renaissance, 10, 227n
McClure, Michael, 32
        "A Statement on Poetics," 76
McLaughlin, John,
        "Interview with Clayton Eshleman," 188, 233n
Measure, 82
Melville, Herman, 10
Merwin, W. S., 37, 228n
Medea, 225
Millet, Kate,
        Sexual Politics, 130
Motherwell, Robert, 136, 137
Mottram, Eric, 228n

Neruda, Pablo, 46, 83, 88
        Residence on Earth, 45, 228n
Neumann, Erich, 147
        The Origins and History of Consciousness, 92, 230n
Nixon, Richard M., 128

Odyssey, 177
Olmstead, Michael S., 228n
Olson, Charles, 9, 10, 11, 24, 29, 32, 46, 51, 69, 72, 75, 80, 81, 95,
    98, 99, 100, 103, 112, 120, 122, 141, 146, 153, 175, 182–183, 184,
    185, 227n
        Call Me Ishmael, 27, 96
        "Fable for Slumber," 18
        "Human Universe," 41
        In Cold Hell, In Thicket, 153
        "The Kingfishers," 33, 95, 119, 156, 182, 229n
        The Maximus Poems, 122, 182, 231n
        Mayan Letters, 51, 229n
        "Projective Verse," 72, 81
        "Proprioception," 146
        "Song of Ullikumi," 156
        The Special View of History, 112
Ono, Yoko, 37
Oppen, George, 31

Origin, 37, 45, 46, 82
Ortiz, Alfonso, 44
Owens, Rochelle, 33, 115, 225, 228n, 233n

Pan, 222, 223, 224
Paris Review, 82
Parker, Charlie, 58
Paz, Octavio, 75, 227n
    The Bow and the Lyre, 17, 227n
Pearce, Donald, 13
Persephone, 106, 204, 218, 223, 225
Petersen, Will, 114
Pollock, Jackson, 142
Postmodernism, 11, 24–27, 32, 54–57, 70–75, 80–82, 112, 137–38
Pound, Ezra, 29, 31, 32, 35, 50, 71, 83, 100, 120, 177, 180, 221, 223
    The Cantos, 177, 180
Powell, Bud, 58, 101, 102, 103, 104, 119
Presley, Elvis, 136
Proust, Marcel, 147, 161

Rabelais, 59, 61, 190, 191
Radin, Paul, 44
Reagan, Ronald, 224
Reich, Wilhelm, 54, 69, 105, 107, 109, 118, 131, 132, 136, 139, 140,
    141, 185, 192, 192
    The Mass Psychology of Fascism, 130, 232n
Religion, 49–53, 59–60, 61–62, 170–71, 184–89, 193, 206–07
Rilke, Rainer Maria, 110
Rimbaud, Arthur, 14, 31, 57, 200
Roosevelt, Franklin D., 128, 183, 184
Rosset, Barney, 82
Rothenberg, Diane, 37, 41, 227n
Rothenberg, Jerome, 10, 32, 33, 34, 35, 36, 37, 46, 85, 125, 137,
    166, 170, 184, 225, 228n, 231n, 233n
        "Cok Boy," 225
        Poems from the Floating World, 34
        Poland 1931, 115
        Ritual, 38, 228n
        Shaking the Pumpkin, 41, 42–43
        Sightings and Lunes, 38
        Symposium of the Whole, 12, 25–26, 41, 44, 125, 227n
        Technicians of the Sacred, 38, 39–40, 44, 228n
        "Vienna Blood," 123
        "Why Deep Image?" 36
Rothko, Mark, 137

Salinger, J. D.,
    The Catcher in the Rye, 79, 229n
Schwerner, Armand, 10, 33, 37, 115, 194, 225, 228n
    The Tablets, 194-95, 225, 233n
Selerie, Gavin, 228n
Shattuck, Roger,
    The Banquet Years, 200-01, 233n
Shepard, Sam,
    The Unseen Hand, 151, 232n
Silva, Ramon Medina, 44
Smart, Christopher, 117
Snyder, Gary, 26, 28, 44, 66, 75, 125, 184, 228n
    "The Politics of Ethnopoetics," 40
Solt, Leo, 46
Solt, Mary Ellen, 46
Soutine, Chaim, 108, 119, 120, 123, 124, 191, 221
St. Anthony, 152, 207
St. Augustine,
    The Confessions, 207
Stead, C. K., 232n
Steinbeck, John, 182
Stevens, Wallace, 51
    "The Snowman," 203

Tasso, 207
Tedlock, Dennis, 26
Thoreau, Henry David, 10
Trobar, 34, 35, 36, 37, 45, 46, 82
Turner, Frederick Jackson, 143
Turner, Victor, 12, 26, 27, 43
True, David, 224
Truman, Harry S, 27, 183

Underworld, 61-69, 123, 177-81, 190-200, 204-07, 211-14

Vallejo, César, 19, 31, 49, 51, 52, 54, 57, 69, 75, 88, 90, 91, 94, 95,
    97, 99, 110, 185, 186, 187, 188
    Battles in Spain, 190
    The Complete Posthumous Poetry, 190, 232n
    Poemas humanos, 97, 99, 100, 110, 230n
    Spain, Take this Cup from Me, 190
Van Gogh, Vincent, 57, 157
Vendler, Helen, 74
Vico, Giovanni Battista, 12

Wainhouse, David,
    Remnants of Empire, 132–34, 232n
Wakoski, Diane, 10, 34, 37, 46, 85, 115, 164, 166, 225, 228n, 232n,
    233n
    Smudging, 165
Wallace, Alfred Russell, 178
Whitehead, Alfred North,
    Process and Reality, 72, 229n
Whitman, Walt, 10, 34, 83, 120
    Leaves of Grass, 100
Wieners, John, 82
Williams, William Carlos, 31, 46, 51, 71
Wilson, Edmund, 200
Wright, James, 188, 288n

Young, Lamont, 37
Youth, 33, 77–79, 127–30, 135–37, 142–45
Yugen, 37, 45

Zukofsky, Louis, 31, 45, 46

Printed April 1991 in Santa Barbara & Ann
Arbor for the Black Sparrow Press by Graham
Mackintosh & Edwards Brothers Inc. Text set in
Century Book by Words Worth. Design by Barbara Martin.
This edition is published in paper wrappers;
there are 300 hardcover trade copies;
100 hardcover copies have been numbered & signed
by the author; & 26 copies handbound in boards by
Earle Gray have been lettered & signed by the author.

96

Photo: Malcolm Quantrill

PAUL CHRISTENSEN was born in Pennsylvania in 1943, and studied with the poet Daniel Hoffman at the University of Pennsylvania, where he earned his doctorate in 1975. He is a professor of literature at Texas A & M University. Among his books of poetry are *Signs of the Whelming* (Latitudes, 1983), *Weights and Measures* (University Editions, 1985), and a new collection, *Earth and World.* His prose includes *Charles Olson: Call Him Ishmael* (University of Texas, 1979), *In Love, In Sorrow: The Complete Correspondence of Charles Olson and Edward Dahlberg* (Paragon House, 1990), and *Minding the Underworld: Clayton Eshleman and Late Postmodernism* (1991). He was a senior Fulbright lecturer to Austria in 1989/90 and a recipient of an N.E.A. poetry grant in 1991.